OSCAR ROMERO

People of God

Remarkable Lives, Heroes of Faith

People of God is a series of inspiring biographies for the general reader. Each volume offers a compelling and honest narrative of the life of an important twentieth- or twenty-first-century Catholic. Some living and some now deceased, each of these women and men has known challenges and weaknesses familiar to most of us but responded to them in ways that call us to our own forms of heroism. Each offers a credible and concrete witness of faith, hope, and love to people of our own day.

More titles to follow

Oscar Romero

Love Must Win Out

Kevin Clarke

LITURGICAL PRESS
Collegeville, Minnesota

www.litpress.org

Cover design by Stefan Killen Design. Cover illustration by Philip Bannister.

1   2   3   4   5   6   7   8   9

Library of Congress Control Number: 2014930907

ISBN 978-0-8146-3757-9

For my parents, Andrew and Maureen Clarke, with all my love and gratitude. And for my own "Romero," Eoin Romero Clarke, with all my hope. My beloved son: keep the faith, build the kingdom.

"Let us not tire of preaching love; it is the force that will overcome the world. Let us not tire of preaching love. Though we see the waves of violence succeed in drowning the fire of Christian love, love must win out; it is the only thing that can." —September 25, 1977

Contents

Acknowledgments

I have to acknowledge in gratitude the many biographers and chroniclers of Archbishop Oscar Romero and the experiences of the people of El Salvador I have relied upon—but particularly the late James Brockman, SJ, María López Vigil, Dean Brackley, SJ, Carlos Dada, and Jon Sobrino, SJ. I would like to acknowledge with love and affection the superior patience and scheduling abilities of my wife Megan, and I would like to hereby apologize to my children, Eoin, Aidan, Ellie and Declan, for the months of absentee parenting and outbursts of stress-induced lunacy to which they were occasionally subjected during the many months and weekends devoted to bringing this book to life.

I would like to thank my co-workers at *America* for their support and encouragement, especially Kerry Weber, James Martin, SJ, and Matt Malone, SJ. I have to also thank the team at Liturgical Press, especially J. Andrew Edwards and Barry Hudock for their patience, encouragement, and for once or twice nudging me away from the ledge.

Introduction

During one of his trips to Rome after his elevation to archbishop of San Salvador, Oscar Romero marveled at how the men in the Curia, indeed it seemed throughout Rome, did not quite understand the nature of the crucifixion being experienced by the church in Latin America, even after his repeated efforts to make these mortal difficulties plain to them. After a humiliating effort to wade through a curial bureaucracy that seemed intent on thwarting him, Romero finally had the chance to meet privately with Pope John Paul II in 1979. He detailed the extreme conditions of his ministry and the human rights violations being inflicted on average Salvadorans, especially church workers. Romero was treated to a few expressions of support but mostly to a good scolding on the importance of maintaining episcopal unity before the eyes of the public.[1] Several of his subordinate bishops in El Salvador at that time were more or less in open revolt against his leadership.

In his diary account of the meeting, Romero writes, "He acknowledged that pastoral work is very difficult in a political climate like the one in which I have to work. He recommended great balance and prudence . . . He reminded me of his situation in Poland, where he was faced with a government that was not Catholic and where he had to develop the church in spite of the difficulties. He said the unity of the bishops is very important. . . . Again I clarified, telling him that this is also something that I want very much, but that I was aware that unity cannot be pretended. Rather, it must be based on the gospel and on the truth."

Pope John Paul II had been receiving numerous reports from within the Salvadoran bishops' conference full of accusations against the archbishop. Now closing out the meeting, Pope John Paul II suggested to Romero that "to resolve the deficiencies in the pastoral work and the lack of harmony among the bishops" an apostolic administrator *sede plena* be appointed, meaning that Romero would remain archbishop of San Salvador but that the actual responsibilities of the position would be moved to the administrator.

Romero apparently accepted the suggestion without protest and "left, pleased by the meeting, but worried to see how much the negative reports of my pastoral work had influenced [the pope]. . . . I think that the audience and our conversation were very useful because he was very frank. I have learned that one cannot expect always to get complete approval, and that it is more useful to hear criticism that can be used to improve our work." A remarkably cool accounting of the meeting, perhaps for posterity's sake, considering Pope John Paul II was essentially proposing to cut the episcopal legs out from under Romero and throw everything he had accomplished into turmoil.[2]

But how could people in Rome and Washington or even in San Vicente understand what Romero understood as the leader of the Salvadoran church? They did not have the spiritual guidance from the Salvadorans that Romero had been receiving for years. He had by then come to believe that the poor were the prophets of the era, not the bishops of El Salvador or the clerical bureaucrats in San Salvador or within the Curia. He was learning from the poor and the oppressed how to be a good Christian in the contemporary milieu of El Salvador and struggling to impart his learning to the elite and powerful in El Salvador and North America and among his superiors in the old world.

This was not mere rhetoric to Romero. He had sat on the ground for impromptu Bible study among El Salvador's campesinos. He had visited with them in parish meeting halls, listening to their interpretation of Scripture and marveling at what he, the esteemed bishop, was learning about the nature of God and faith from the ignored and the oppressed. Yes, he heard the desperate cry of the poor for justice in El Salvador, but more than that he heard wisdom from the poor—unexpected prophets—that many simply refused to hear.

That unwillingness to hear persisted far longer than Romero could have imagined. Perhaps it awaited clarity from one whose experience more closely mirrored his own, someone who brought not only a fresh perspective but a personal familiarity with the contradictions and cruelties of life in some of the far-flung corners of Christendom. Perhaps it awaited the right ears for the hearing.

It had been a fantastic hope of the Catholic faithful of Latin America that one day one of their own should become Bishop of Rome and represent the perspective and experience of this largest population of Catholics in the world before the rest of their Catholic brothers and sisters. That hope was finally realized in the humble form of Argentina's Cardinal Jorge Mario Bergoglio, who has become fondly known to the world as Pope Francis.

Soon after his election in April 2013, Pope Francis stepped into one of those occasional—and inexplicable to outsiders—disagreements that trouble somber Vatican corridors in what would become typical of his direct and empathetic style. Pope Francis "unblocked" the canonization process for Servant of God—declared so in 1997 by Pope John Paul II—and servant of the people of El Salvador, Oscar Romero.

Given the complex of concerns that collide over the notion of the canonization of this martyred archbishop, perhaps this definitive moment had to wait for a man like Cardinal Bergoglio to fully appreciate the life, wisdom, and sacrifice of Oscar Romero, to understand the nature of his sainthood and of his world. As a young man rushed into a position of authority during a period of grave national crisis, one for which he later acknowledged he did not believe himself ready, then Father Bergoglio vividly experienced the historical, spiritual, and psychological torrents that pulled apart the people of Latin America during the waning decades of the twentieth century.

Archbishop Romero and Pope Francis seem to follow parallel spiritual and practical tracks. Although not a member of the Society of Jesus as Cardinal Bergoglio had been before he became pontiff, Romero had been taught by Jesuits and was a graduate of the Jesuits' Pontifical Gregorian University in Rome. He had deep experience with and profound respect for Ignatian spirituality and had undertaken the Ignatian Spiritual Exercises himself as a young man.

Both men, perhaps owing to their Jesuit spiritual training, shared an understanding of the practical implications of "seeking God in all things," a sense of openness to the work of God in history and the world, including in struggle and discord. After his elevation to archbishop, surveying the crying needs of his community, Romero could not conceive of closing off the Salvadoran church behind a wall of showy ritual and pious observations while forces of economic and political oppression swirled around it. He sought to engage the church in its times and its concerns. As Pope Francis has said, what good is a closed-off church? He exhorts a church that embraces the messiness of life, its joys and sorrows, and speaks of a church as a social triage, a hospital where the spiritually wounded find succor. There were times in Romero's life when that image of church was no metaphor, but an everyday reality.

In good Jesuit fashion, Romero was a believer in discussion and discernment, though he surely had his moments of authoritarian decision-making. Some of his most dramatic gestures and decisions as archbishop, for example, the pivotal decision to conduct only one Mass across the nation on the Sunday following the assassination of Rutilio Grande, came after lengthy consultation with other priests and carefully weighing many opinions. Perhaps most tellingly, Romero did not give his own sensibilities and concerns any particular extra weight in balance against the opinions of others. Through such discernment and consultation, he was able to overcome the limits his own conservative instincts and inclinations might have placed on his perspective and field of operation.

Romero warned repeatedly of idolatries, whether of social privilege, an inherited and presumptive economic order, or Marxist contradictions of it. He frequently sought wisdom about such matters in the lives of the poor whom he loved. "The poor person is the one who has been converted to God and puts all his faith in him," he said, "and the rich person is one who has not been converted to God and puts his confidence in idols: money, power, material things. . . . All of our work should be directed toward converting ourselves and all people to this authentic meaning of poverty. For Christ said that the secret is this: You cannot serve two masters, God and mammon."[3]

Cardinal Jorge chose to name himself after Francis of Assisi because the twelfth-century saint was a man of peace, a man who "loves and protects creation," but perhaps most of all a man of poverty, a person who knew its depravities and ingenuities, its oppression and its joys. "How I would like a church that is poor and for the poor," Pope Francis said just days after his election.

Oscar Romero, a defender of the poor, a voice for the voiceless, was someone who intimately understood the joy and liberation of a church that is poor, that is of the poor and that is for the poor. After he began his lonely course of resistance to the Salvadoran status quo, Romero was abandoned by just about all of his brother bishops in El Salvador. He became a pariah to the social caste in Salvador he challenged, an irritant to Salvador's political sponsors in Washington whose geopolitical strategies he threatened to overturn. In the end the poor were all he had left, and they knew it and loved him more for it.

On February 18, 1979, the first Sunday after Romero returned from the Puebla conference in Mexico during which the Latin American bishops had accepted the church's "option for the poor," he said in his homily, "In our preaching to rich and poor, it is not that we pander to the sins of the poor and ignore the virtues of the rich. Both have sins and both need conversion. But the poor, in their condition of need, are disposed to conversion. They are more conscious of their need of God.

"Therefore, if we really want to learn the meaning of conversion and faith, if we want to learn what it means to trust other people, then it is necessary to become poor or, at the very least, it is necessary to make the cause of the poor our own. That is when one begins to experience faith and conversion: when one has the heart of the poor, when one knows that financial capital, political influence, and power are worthless, and that without God we are nothing."[4]

Pope Francis and Archbishop Romero share a striking and sincere simplicity, humility, and modesty that encouraged them to renounce many of the symbolic and practical privileges of their ecclesial positions, right down to the clothing they wore and the means of transportation they employed. Surely they both possess a taste for modest living and a sense that their vocations demanded a life in community, not one that could be endured in practical and psychological isolation. No mean feat for either man.

Pope Francis renounced many of the creature comforts and structural confinements of his position, rejecting the regal papal apartments—breaking a tradition that has continued since 1903—to accept a suite in the Santa Marta Residence, the Vatican's modern guesthouse for priests and bishops who work in the Roman Curia or are visiting the Vatican for meetings and conferences. This choice was a practical reflection of his desire to adopt a simple living arrangement allowing him to live in community with other priests and bishops. In a similar way, instead of accepting the offer of an extravagant manse upon his elevation to archbishop, Romero elected to live in the sacristy of the Divine Providence Hospital and later accepted a small domicile on the cancer center's grounds. He celebrated his last eucharistic sacrifice at its modest chapel. Such simplicity was liberating for both men, allowing them to speak their hearts and minds with legitimacy and authority because that legitimacy and that authority has been earned by the lives they led and the joyful and loving example they set.

Both men delight in the people; they feel a deep and sincere need to be among the people. "The people are my prophet," Romero said, and "with a people like this, it's not hard to be a good shepherd." At his elevation to the papacy, Pope Francis's first act was not to offer the traditional blessing to those gathered to see the new pontiff in St. Peter's Square. Instead, with fear and trepidation appropriate to the great responsibility before him, Pope Francis asked for their blessing upon him. The startled crowd responded with a prayer and a roar of approval. Likewise on the night of Rutilio Grande's death, Oscar Romero turned to the assembled faithful during an impromptu 4:00 a.m. Mass, feeling the sudden realization of the awful burden he was about to accept, the threshold he was about to cross as a mournful dawn approached. "I want to . . . ask for your prayers," he said, "that I be faithful to this promise, that I will not abandon my people. Rather, I will run with them all the risks that my ministry demands."[5]

Romero used the acclaim and attention he provoked among the people at Mass in the Metropolitan Cathedral as a job performance gauge. He drew sustenance and courage from their affection, offered and reciprocated. Today Pope Francis has succeeded in nearly doubling the television viewership of his daily angelus homilies. To the consternation of his Swiss Guards, he has restored baby-kissing as a political and ecclesial art form, blithely rejecting the thick glass of the Popemobile, which may offer personal safety but contributes to a distance he recognizes as spiritually isolating. Romero rejected the offer of military bodyguards both as a political gesture of resistance to the government—fully appreciating the cynicism of the government's offer of "help"—but also as an expression of solidarity with the Salvadoran people. "I don't want protection as long as my people are not given protection," he said. "With them, I want to run all the risks that my vocation demands of me."

Both men had been considered conservative, bookish, withdrawn. But now Francis proclaims he was never the "rightist" that some took him to be, though in his too-youthful appointment to provincial, his authoritarianism, driven by insecurity, may have suggested it to some people. Romero, considered a "safe" appointment during a time of class and social uproar in El Salvador, proved that age had not calcified his vision or reduced his consciousness into a hard, lifeless thing. Both men have demonstrated the powerful works that liberation and joy and courage can achieve.

Given the many parallels they embody as pastors and as men drawn from Latin America's peculiar and sometimes cruel intersection of history, race, and faith, perhaps it is not so surprising that one of Pope Francis's first acts of ecclesial daring was to push for the unblocking of the canonization of a fellow prelate from the New World, known to him to be beloved of his people.

Why was such unblocking necessary? It wasn't until 1993 that Romero's cause was first opened in El Salvador, but Romero's orthodoxy and loyalty to the church were not "confirmed" until July 2005, after a review by the Congregation for the Doctrine of Faith that had continued for years.[6] More than thirty years after his assassination, those devoted to "San Romero" still await his formal canonization.

The church traditionally has limited the status of martyrdom to those who are killed after refusing to renounce their faith or those murdered explicitly because they are Catholic. Romero's martyrdom was clearly of a different sort. Was Romero a political or a spiritual martyr? Did his faith or his politics propel him to this death before the altar?

Powerful people in El Salvador and in Rome have quietly campaigned against his sainthood, arguing that Romero did not die for his faith or for the poor, but as a "combatant" in a political struggle, worse, a social antagonist who contributed to public disorder. During his lifetime, Romero endured scoldings at home and in Rome for seeming to choose sides in El Salvador. Powerful bishops within his own conference condemned the archbishop, and after his death opposed the cause for his sainthood, seeing in it an indictment of their role and the side they elected to defend during El Salvador's years of torment. Romero's cause for sainthood wasn't helped when in death he became the unofficial symbol of those on the left in El Salvador who had taken up the armed resistance.

The anniversaries of his martyrdom have come and gone, and each March as it approaches, advocates for Romero's sainthood have waited in hope for official word that this man would become a saint. Up to now they have waited in vain. In 2007 Pope Benedict XVI said that the archbishop was "certainly a great witness of the faith" who "merits beatification, I do not doubt." (Words that were later absurdly stricken from the official transcript though they were spoken before a planeload of journalists.) He explained that obstacles had been thrown before Romero's cause, however, when some groups unjustly tried to co-opt Romero as a political figure.

During the final years of his life, Archbishop Romero became a touchstone of hope for the oppressed of El Salvador and a lightning rod of resentment among its ruling elite. In speaking the truth of Christian faith to the military and economic elite of El Salvador—and not coincidently the United States—Romero could not help but stir up controversy and outrage among those whose privileges he challenged. Romero was among one of the better-cataloged clerics of his time. Just about every one of his public appearances as archbishop was captured by international and local television and radio news. He chronicled his own thoughts as a weekly contributor to his diocesan paper; his homilies were broadcast live and quickly transcribed; his weekly radio addresses captivated the nation. Is it possible for someone sifting through such a collection of one individual's words, from newspaper columns to impulsive comments on the street, to find comments that can be construed as political or inflammatory? Did Romero not speak of "revolution" at times as if urging it on?

The truth is he did, and at certain impassioned moments, the archbishop probably said things he might have wished he had phrased differently, in a manner more attuned to the political nuances at home and curial intrigues in Rome. Romero's more passionate comments were enough for some to use to denigrate—and imperil—him during his life. They were enough later for some to use to stand in the way of the cause for the sainthood of Oscar Romero.

But in those few instances when Romero used political terms such as *revolution* or *struggle*, in his own heart Romero was thinking of a different kind of struggle, a different kind of revolution surely than the ones imagined by the emerging armed resistance within El Salvador. Ultimately the revolution that Romero spoke of is the kind that can be experienced by all—not one that is manifest in class struggle, but one manifest in the heart and the head, a revolution of spirit that overcomes both the oppressor and the oppressed and makes such terms meaningless.

Was Romero political? Yes, he certainly was. He came to understand the social struggle in El Salvador as a political conflict, and in that struggle he sided with the poor and insisted that the church do the same. But in his eyes this was never a Marxist class struggle, but merely a struggle of people attempting to protect themselves from social and actual violence and establish for themselves a more just and equitable society, free of official impunity and political repression. That meant among the affluent some share of privilege that they were murderously resistant to offering. His job was to attempt to convert them, to persuade them to offer up that privilege as a sacrifice that would restore the community.

Romero came to see many Salvadoran revolutionaries not as ideological warriors carrying out a "classic" Marxist struggle but as campesinos and the educated children of campesinos defending their people against sometimes incomprehensible violence and the life-crushing force of economic and social oppression that was specific to the time, geography, and history of Central America. Their *lucha* was not rooted in nineteenth- and early-twentieth-century Europe ideological conflicts, but the historical reality of contemporary Central America. He knew many of them were aroused to resist social injustice not by Marxist dogma but by the teaching of the church itself. Did he support the revolutionaries? Even as he criticized some of the violence of the revolutionary forces within El Salvador and worried over their tactics, he did in general support them in the same way he supported the right of a vulnerable person to self-defense and of a hungry man to steal food to feed his family. But these last beliefs were based not on Marxist dialectics, but Catholic catechism. Romero was able to discern the difference; many of his detractors, mired in Europe and the Cold War, were not. Their imaginations were too frozen by the church's long struggle with communism to understand that not all revolutions and revolutionaries are created equal.

In 2010 on the thirtieth anniversary of Romero's death, when many thought Romero's beatification would surely be announced, San Salvador Archbishop José Luis Escobar explained the stalled process as the result of efforts by some to "manipulate, politicize or use Romero's image."[7] The cause of Romero's sainthood had been held up because of concerns among some powerful bishops that Romero's canonization would signal the church's approval of liberation theology, a controversial convergence of Scripture interpretation and Marxist social critique that has long made some clerics, those perhaps most comfortable with the status quo in Latin America, uneasy.

It is no doubt a concern that would have amused the late archbishop. Romero himself had once been one of those cautious clerics and sought to temper the stridency of the some proponents of liberation theology. He understood the need, and the difficulty, in maintaining a balance between advocacy for the vulnerable and the oppressed and outright political partisanship. As a result, for every Catholic "rightist" in El Salvador who grew furious at the bishop for his defense of the defenseless, a Catholic "leftist" could be found ready to denounce the bishop's timidity. It says more about the politics of the Curia over the last three decades than it does about Archbishop Romero's actual beliefs and spiritual focus that his sainthood should have been stymied for so long over this concern.

But there are other ways for sainthood to be confirmed. Few among the people who knew and loved him personally have needed Rome's seal of approval to embrace Romero as a saint. Three days after his assassination, an attorney for the archdiocese was preparing the Monseñor's death certificate with employees of the San Salvador municipal bureaucracy. "Could it be we are about to bury a saint?" they asked the attorney.[8]

Few among the poor and oppressed of El Salvador have had to wonder about Romero's sainthood. And over the years as thousands of Catholics all over the world learn about Romero and his legacy of conviction and courage, no official word has been necessary to confirm his saintliness.

The people of El Salvador have already declared their saint; he has never been "blocked" on the streets of San Salvador and in the deepest precincts of the heart where true saint-hood resides.

The people's proclamation of Romero's sainthood may not pass a formal review in Rome, but it is not dissimilar to the manner that saints were elevated during the church's first thousand years when it was the people, not the prelates, who discerned the sainthood of the beloved departed. During Romero's funeral, which turned into a bloodbath itself as security elements attacked those who had come to mourn the martyred archbishop, the devotion and affection that the people of El Salvador maintained for their archbishop was already evident. Now each year thousands march on the anniversary of his death, at times they have done so at great peril, in a statement of resistance that is also a defiant gesture of devotion and a declaration of a popular embrace of Romero's sainthood. That elevation, a canonization by the people, would undoubtedly be all that Romero could have wished for.

CHAPTER ONE

Death Comes for the Archbishop

No one may have noticed the red Volkswagen Passat as it glided slowly to a stop near the modest chapel of the Divine Providence Hospital. Two other cars haunted the streets outside the small church: one filled with armed men working as "security" for the assassin and, in the other car, two men who loosely supervised the operation waited to assess its outcome.

A thin, bearded man, the Passat's passenger and a stranger to its driver Amado Garay, told Garay to crouch down and pretend to repair something.[1]

On another typically hot evening in San Salvador, the Carmelite sisters had kindly left the wing-shaped chapel doors open, hoping for a breath of air to cool the congregants inside. Through the open doors of the Divine Providence Chapel the assassin had a clear view of Archbishop Oscar Romero at the altar as he made his way through the homily he had prepared for this requiem Mass, one he agreed to celebrate for the mother of a friend. "My dear sisters and brothers," the archbishop was saying, his homily gathering steam. "I think we should not only pray this

15

evening for the eternal rest of our dear Doña Sarita, but above all we should take to ourselves her message . . . that every Christian ought to want to live intensely. Many do not understand; they think Christianity should not be involved in such things," Archbishop Romero said, referring to the "things" of the physical world, the problems of the times in which we live. "But, to the contrary," he continued, "you have just heard in Christ's gospel that one must not love oneself so much as to avoid getting involved in the risks of life that history demands of us and that those who try to fend off the danger will lose their lives, while those who out of love for Christ give themselves to the service of others, will live, live like the grain of wheat that dies, but only apparently. If it did not die, it would remain alone." He was wrapping up yet another memorable homily for those gathered in the church and those who would listen to his words later on the radio. "The harvest comes about," he said, "only because it dies, allowing itself to be sacrificed in the earth and destroyed. Only by undoing itself does it produce the harvest."[2]

Soon he would elevate the host above the altar, and he would speak the words of transfiguration; his eyes, as so many hundreds of times before, would be on the host held high before him. If for a second then he had glanced through the open doors of the chapel, would he have seen the young man taking aim? Would he have been afraid? Would he have been tempted to flee? It hardly matters. We know Archbishop Romero was focused on prayer at the moment of his death, preparing for that prayer said during the Eucharist at Masses each day all over the world. We know also that as he spoke his last homily the archbishop knew that death was seeking him out; he knew his words were pulling death closer to him. He surely knew, too, that if he were only to remain silent, to stop speaking out about the killing and the oppression and the poverty, death just might lose interest in him. There were so many others on death lists in El Salvador in those days on whom it could slake its thirst. But Romero would not be silent.

"Dear brothers and sisters," he said in this final homily, his final moments, "let us all view these matters at this historic moment with [hope], that spirit of giving and of sacrifice. Let us all do what we can. . . . because all those longings for justice, peace, and well-being that we experience on earth become realized for us if we enlighten them with Christian hope. We know that no one can go on forever, but those who have put into their work a sense of very great faith, of love of God . . . find it all results in the splendors of a crown that is the sure reward of those who labor thus, cultivating truth, justice, love, and goodness on earth. Such labor does not remain here below but, purified by God's Spirit, is harvested for our reward."[3]

Outside in the red Passat, Garay heard a shot, turned around and saw his anonymous passenger "holding a gun with both hands pointing towards the right side of the rear right window of the vehicle." Garay could smell gunpowder. The bearded man turned to him and calmly told him, "Drive slowly, take it easy." He did as he was asked; no one interfered with the assassins as they departed. The two men drove in silence to meet with the supervisors of the operation. "Mission accomplished," the thin, bearded man told them.

Everyone in El Salvador who could reach a radio or visit with the monseñor in person at Mass listened to Romero's homilies. His words brought hope and courage to thousands. But to some who listened—just as intently—they only provoked a cold, seething hatred. Romero's homily was "the little morsel for the day all over," as one of the conspirators in the archbishop's murder would remember later. Everyone tuned in for them: the poor, the workers, the revolutionaries, surely, but also the leaders of the death squads and the members of the business and landowning class alarmed by the growing social consciousness of El Salvador's peasants. "They used to say that Romero's homily, that he was the one who was stirring people up," one of the conspirators remembers.[4]

On the night he was murdered, there was much celebrating among the military and members of El Salvador's patron class, those who had ordered the killing of the archbishop and those who were merely cheered to discover it had taken place. There was much contentment on a farm in Santa Tecla, where Salvadoran anticommunist leader Roberto D'Aubuisson had been waiting with a group of his followers to hear the outcome of the operation. But thirty years later, few of those directly responsible would feel like celebrating. D'Aubuisson was dead—killed by cancer of the tongue—as were many of those directly involved in the assassination of the archbishop, some under highly suspicious circumstances. Perhaps there remain a few who are happy to have their role in Romero's death whispered only to the grave. The man who pulled the trigger, in fact, has never been caught.

Captain Álvaro Rafael Saravia was among those who celebrated the night of March 24, 1980, but his delight was to be short-lived. One of the few direct conspirators today still among the living, his experience since the Salvadoran peace sputtered into life in 1992 has been one of exile and diminishment. But back then, as one of D'Aubuisson's most trusted lieutenants, he could only have been gratified about how well the "operation" had turned out, how professionally it had been conducted.

He had long been suspected of being the man in the Passat, the man who pulled the trigger. But, tracked down after years devoted to hiding himself in the United States and Central America in flight from a civil judgment against him for the killing of Romero, Saravia is finally ready to come clean, to tell what happened that night. His role in the killing of the archbishop and many other people over the years of El Salvador's civil war has cost him dearly. After resigning his commission as an officer in the Salvadoran military in 1979, by 1985 he had left his homeland, abandoning his family. He first escaped to the United States in 1985. He soon went underground to escape a criminal court case; he had been suspected of laundering money for Colombian drug traffickers. Far from the days of his pride and glory as a Salvadoran air force officer, he worked in the United States as a pizza deliveryman and then a used-car salesman in Modesto, California. His final escape, this time into the international ether, began after a civil case was initiated against him for Romero's murder by the Center for Justice and Accountability in San Francisco.

After running for so long from Romero's assassination, Saravia is happy to set the record straight when he is brought to ground by Carlos Dada, a founding editor and investigative reporter from El Salvador's *El Faro*, a digital newspaper.

"You wrote this, right?" Saravia says, referring to an article that speculated that Saravia himself had pulled the trigger that felled the archbishop. "Well it's wrong. . . . It says here, 'Several years after murdering Archbishop Romero.' And I didn't kill him."

"Who killed him then? Someone from outside El Salvador?" Dada questioned. "No," said Saravia. "An 'indio,' one of our own. He's still out there somewhere." Was Saravia denying that he had a role in Romero's murder?

"Thirty years and this is going to persecute me until I die," Saravia mutters to the journalist. "Of course I participated. That's why we're here talking."[5]

Ironically because of the hell he is living in, an impoverished exile from history and from his own people, even from his own family (his children "look at me as if I'm Hitler," he mournfully explains to Dada), Saravia has nothing but sympathy now for the men and women he once hunted in El Salvador as "communists." And of course for himself.

Look at me now, he implores the reporter who has tracked him down to this poor farming community in Central America. "If I could do something for these people some day, I'd do it. Even take up arms. I've suffered alongside these people: So there's no corn. Go pick some bananas then. Sometimes there's corn, but nothing to go with it. So you have to put salt on the tortillas. . . . And sometimes there isn't even that.

"There's a family living across from me. Sometimes they give me four tortillas or so. And if that's being a communist . . . it's communist. It would have been communist to [D'Aubuisson] in those days. Take him out, wreck his house, and tell him 'sonofabitch, you're with the guerrillas.' " The irony of these late political epiphanies is not lost on Saravia. "How would a man not become a guerrilla when he's watching his children die of hunger?" he says. "I'd grab my gun and go straight into hell. I wouldn't hesitate three seconds . . . It wouldn't take much to convince me."[6]

The man he helped kill can be said to have unknowingly set upon the path to martyrdom on February 17, 1980, when he addressed a letter to President Jimmy Carter pleading that the American president not send military aid to the Salvadoran government. Romero warned President Carter that whatever material support the United States provided would quickly be turned against the people of El Salvador themselves. That gesture was provocative enough, but the archbishop would soon generate even deeper animus among the men who held his life and death in their hands.

The night before his murder, Romero made a personal appeal in a desperate attempt to place some sort of moral obstacle before the escalating pace of the killing in El Salvador. He spoke directly to those soldiers of the night who were most responsible for the growing horror. "I would like to appeal in a special way to the men of the Army," he said, "and in particular to the troops of the National Guard, the police, and the garrisons. Brothers, you belong to our own people. You kill your own brother peasants; and in the face of an order to kill that is given by a man, the law of God that says 'Do not kill!' should prevail. No soldier is obliged to obey an order counter to the law of God. No one has to comply with an immoral law. It is time now that you recover your conscience and obey its dictates rather than the command of sin. . . . Therefore, in the name of God, and in the name of this long-suffering people, whose laments rise to heaven every day more tumultuous, I beseech you, I beg you, I command you! In the name of God: 'Cease the repression!'"

The applause was so thunderous the radio station's beleaguered audio technicians at first took it for some sort of short circuit or feedback in the system that had knocked the good archbishop off the air. But that hadn't happened; it was only the thundering endorsement of the assembly. Romero's words had been heard by all.

For Romero to have said such words after receiving so many warnings and direct threats is a testament to his faith and his courage. As far as the men who were directing the violence against the "leftists" in El Salvador were concerned, Romero was speaking the purest blasphemy to the soldiers.

They understood how the bishop's words threatened their tenuous authority and control of these men. Many of El Salvador's "professional" military were young men drawn from the peasant communities they were ordered to assault—as Romero noted it was their own brothers and sisters they were abusing, even murdering. Worse, many had been informally "conscripted" off the streets in strong-arm recruitments that were essentially kidnappings. Could such brutalized, unwilling men be relied upon to dispense, on command, so much brutality themselves? And against their own people? The anxious doubt many of the elite in the officers' ranks already maintained and now stoked by the words of the archbishop, was proving unbearable. Could someone not shut this priest up?

Salvadoran newspapers that supported the junta had already essentially called for Romero's assassination. They had condemned him as "a demagogic and violent archbishop" who "preached terrorism from his cathedral." One menaced, "The armed forces should begin to oil their weapons."

And just two weeks before he was shot through the heart, a briefcase containing an unexploded bomb was found behind the pulpit of the church where, the day before, he had said Mass for a murdered government official. The day of his final Mass, a large advertisement announced his schedule for that evening and his attendance as celebrant at the requiem. Romero cheerfully dismissed the concerns a diocesan staff member raised about the unusually prominent announcement.

He must have known they were coming for him and that it was too late to turn back. He certainly knew that death was stalking him. Since the killing of his dear friend, the Jesuit Rutilio Grande, Romero understood where the path that he was following would lead.

Though he dismissed the concerns of others, he was acutely aware that he could be preparing the ground for his own martyrdom, and he knew in all likelihood that his death would be violent. He had already seen what had become of many who had threatened the political order in El Salvador, and that specter of his own fate filled him with dread as it would any person. Romero loved life; he loved his people. He was not eager to leave either behind. Despite all he faced, Romero remained acutely attentive to nurturing and safeguarding his spiritual life to the end. In his last retreat, he made a note of one of his final discussions with his spiritual director. "My other fear is for my life. It is not easy to accept a violent death, which is very possible in these circumstances, and the apostolic nuncio to Costa Rica warned me of imminent danger just this week. You have encouraged me, reminding me that my attitude should be to hand my life over to God regardless of the end to which that life might come; that unknown circumstances can be faced with God's grace; that God assisted the martyrs, and that if it comes to this I shall feel God very close as I draw my last breath; but that more valiant than surrender in death is the surrender of one's whole life—a life lived for God."[7]

US Ambassador Robert White heard Romero's March 23 "Cease the repression" sermon in person, surrounded at Mass by his own security detail. Because of his attentiveness to human rights issues, White was also considered suspect by the subterranean right-wing forces and had his own share of death threats with which to contend. "I really worried about him and his forthrightness," White recalled twenty-four years later as a civil trial in California began in an effort to flush out the Romero conspirators. "There were limits to how far you could go," White said. "I would have preferred that he would have been more prudent."[8]

Certainly there were men in El Salvador the night before Romero's death who heard Romero's imploring words to the soldiers in the streets of her cities and the hills of her countryside who knew exactly what Romero was doing with those last words. He was signing his own death warrant. The men of the death squads had long ago gotten over whatever superstitions they might have had about killing a priest. Now they were ready to kill a bishop, even one standing before an altar.

What does one need to kill an archbishop? It did not take a lot to plan a murder in those days with so many people and materials already on hand to do the job. The author of Romero's murder, Roberto D'Aubuisson, is suspected of jotting down a brief reminder note found lodged in Saravia's agenda book—a checklist for one operation to kill a priest. Saravia had so many and varied clandestine operations going at the same time, the book was essential for keeping track of his many dark responsibilities. Much of what was revealed by the agenda was known years before by American officials and reported to Washington, according to American diplomats.

These diplomats told *The New York Times* in 1987 that the CIA had been given Saravia's notebook in 1980 or 1981, but failed to follow up on it. When asked why, an American official who served in El Salvador at the time said, "The CIA didn't mind what was going on so long as they were killing Communists."[9]

The book has been called the Rosetta stone of Salvador's bloody conflict. It offers a small window into the dark world inhabited by Saravia, D'Aubuisson, and perhaps thirty other rightist army officers and business people close to D'Aubuisson who had participated in establishing and running death squads in El Salvador.

One of Saravia's assignments was dubbed "Operation Pineapple," a simple op to smuggle in hand grenades from sources in Guatemala—an operation that is suspected of being the cover story for the planning of Romero's assassination. D'Aubuisson's list details the "must haves" for Romero's murder: 1 starlight, 1 257 roberts, 4 automatics, grenades, 1 driver, 1 sniper, 4 security.

The "starlight" is a telescopic sight for a precision rifle. The sniper would have a difficult shot to make: thirty-five meters from the street to the chapel altar. The "257 roberts" refers to a 25-caliber Remington rifle with a telescopic lens frequently used for sharpshooting, but it was probably not the weapon used to kill the archbishop. Romero was killed with a 22-caliber bullet through the heart. Though Saravia called the sniper "one of ours," he was most likely a Nicaraguan, a veteran of the Somoza regime's notorious National Guard. He had been hired for one thousand colones. That would be about four hundred dollars. The four automatics and grenades mentioned on the list would be allocated among the four members of the detail that accompanied the sniper, providing security for the operation.[10]

What else is required to kill an archbishop? The hand of fate, which selected the date and time of Romero's murder. In the early morning hours on the day of the killing, Captain Eduardo Ávila Ávila, one of the conspirators, woke up Saravia and another member of the operation clutching a copy of the daily *La Prensa Gráfica*. Within its pages he had found a divine signal that today was meant to be Romero's last. The Ávila name appeared over and over again throughout a Mass announcement printed in the newspaper. He perceived it as a message, a call to strike.

The Mass had been scheduled to commemorate the first anniversary of the death of Sara Meardi de Pinto. Her son, Jorge Pinto, her grandchildren, and the Kriete-Ávila, Quiñónez-Ávila, González-Ávila, Ávila-Meardi, Aguilar-Ávila, and Ávila-Ávila families had used an advertisement in the paper to extend an invitation "to the Holy Mass that will be officiated by the Archbishop of San Salvador in the Church of Divine Providence Hospital at 6:00 p.m. today." The conspirators had a place and a time and, more important, they had a sign from above. This was the Mass announcement that had worried Romero's coworker.

That evening at the Mass for Doña Sarita, Romero was finishing the homily. "In this chalice the wine is transformed into the blood that was the price of salvation," he told the assembly before him. "May this body immolated and this blood sacrificed for humans nourish us also, so that we may give our body and our blood to suffering and to pain—like Christ, not for self, but to bring about justice and peace for our people."

The instant when a shot cracked the quiet of the church has been captured for eternity on audiotape. The assassin found his target, and Oscar Romero, mortally wounded, tumbled to the floor behind the altar. Some sisters and others at Mass quickly reached his side, indifferent to the possible threat to their own lives as pandemonium erupted in the chapel. But the archbishop was already dead, and the red Passat, with the young man inside, was drifting away into the streets of San Salvador.

CHAPTER TWO

Romero's El Salvador

When biographers tell the story of Archbishop Oscar Romero, the general narrative is of a pious, congenitally cautious man growing increasingly informed and spiritually and politically radicalized by the suffering of the people placed in his care, first as bishop of the Diocese of Santiago de María, then later when he became the archbishop of San Salvador in February 1977. The somewhat conservative cleric is slowly drawn into an awareness of the injustice that surrounds him and the acute suffering of the Salvadoran campesinos before he is snapped into a spiritual awakening to his responsibilities after the murder of his dear friend, the Jesuit Rutilio Grande. This may be described as the legend of "Rutilio's miracle." In this story, Romero, initially considered a safe and conservative choice for archbishop, is quickly transformed into a courageous advocate for the poor, a social critic, and political opponent of the established order by the suffering he witnesses and the misdeeds of shadowy elements from within the Salvadoran government and military.

There is no doubt that some isolation and obliviousness can be encouraged by the clerical life. Romero spent years away from El Salvador during his formation and in many ways he was insulated from day-to-day realities in the countryside by the kind of work he did for the church. There are enough stories of the archbishop's awakening late in life to the unjust conditions endured by the poor and campesinos in El Salvador to suggest there must be some truth to this "awakening to justice" narrative of Romero's last years of life.

And following the murder of his friend Rutilio, the archbishop was indeed moved to bolder action on behalf of the campesinos and the people of El Salvador, but is it possible for Romero not to have more than a passing acquaintance with the conditions of the poor in El Salvador? He grew up among them; his father's work would have put him in intimate contact with them as a boy. As a young man his work as pastor put him directly into the cares of their lives.

And long before he would have been "radicalized," according to the usual narrative of Romero's social awakening, he was already contemplating issues of justice and peace related to the interconnections of Salvadoran society and its economy. In late November 1976 Romero wrote in his regular column in *El Apóstol*, the diocesan weekly that he founded and edited, of the moral implications of the upcoming coffee harvest. "God, always glorious in his works, is giving us this year too that splendid rain of rubies [ripe, red coffee beans] that draws thousands of hands from everywhere to gather the rich gifts of our mountains." But, Romero wrote, "Humans' sin makes the beauty of creation groan," then he turns to a quote from Vatican II's *Gaudium et Spes* (69), "For this reason the church must cry out by God's command: 'God has meant the earth and all it contains for the use of the whole human race. Created wealth should reach all in just form, guided by justice and accompanied by charity. Whatever the form of property-holding, we must not lose sight of this universal purpose of all wealth.' "[1]

In a few short sentences Romero comments on one of the principal forms and causes of oppression of El Salvador's campesinos; though the coffee harvest may have brought riches to some, it often did little to alleviate the hunger and need of El Salvador's poor, but furthered their oppression. Romero, using the words of Vatican II's *Gaudium et Spes*, challenges the social structure that was built on that oppression and the privilege that lurked behind it. He even challenges the sacrosanct nature of private property. Crucially, he makes this challenge without resorting to economic or social theory but relies on Catholic anthropology to make his case about the "universal destination of earthly goods," in this specific case the wealth generated by the coffee harvest.

Even in the weeks before he assumed his new role as archbishop, Romero was offering indications of a mind in movement, alert to the political forces and acts of oppression swirling around the church of El Salvador. In February, in a brief interview in San Salvador's *La Prensa Gráfica*, the soon-to-be archbishop said, "We must keep to the center, watchfully, in the traditional way, but seeking justice." Romero allowed that the mission of a priest is "eminently religious and transcendent," but, he added, "the government should not consider a priest who makes a stand for social justice as a politician or a subversive element when he is fulfilling his mission in the politics of the common good."[2]

"Rutilio's miracle," it appears, was already in motion.

Oscar Arnulfo Romero y Galdámez came into the world in Ciudad Barrios in the department of San Miguel on August 15, 1917. He was born in a town in the eastern part of El Salvador just ten miles from the border with Honduras, but no road connected the community to bigger towns in Honduras or El Salvador or to the wider world then distracted by World War I. The town was unreachable except by horseback or on foot until long after Oscar Romero had grown into manhood.[3]

His father, Santos, was described as "not pious."[4] He and his wife Guadalupe raised seven children (one child died at birth), and Santos was father also to a child, a daughter, with another woman in Ciudad Barrios. He may have been "not pious," but according to Romero in a loving remembrance of his father after he had passed, Santos "would pace the bedroom floor," teaching the boy and, one presumes, his siblings the standard Catholic repertoire of prayers and the Ten Commandments.[5]

Santos worked as the town's postmaster and telegraph operator and maintained the office out of the Romero home. As a child Oscar Romero learned to send and receive telegrams, which surely connected him to the highs and lows of life in a poor, rural community without electricity. His father also worked twenty acres of hillside land that his wife had inherited, growing cacao and coffee like the other campesinos of the community.[6] The children learned to milk the cow. They ran errands for their father such as delivering telegrams around the community. The siblings shared chores and they shared beds—or floor space; the family's material means were modest. His family did have enough to enjoy small pleasures, and as a child Oscar never missed the circus when one made it to Ciudad Barrios.

Romero's siblings remember him as prayerful, too serious, perhaps a little sad, always "turned inward."

"My brother thought too much," one recalled. Like many boys whose hearts and minds were set on the priesthood, as a child Oscar Romero enjoyed playacting as a priest. While other children were running around getting into mischief, Oscar preferred to throw one of his mother's aprons over his head and pretend to lead a procession around the streets near his home, calling out to the neighborhood children and imagining he was already a priest.[7] "He played the role of priest; he would stand on top of the mortar that was used to grind coffee and then take in his hand a brush that was used to paint houses," his brother Tiberio remembered. "He would dip the brush into a bucket filled with water and sprinkle the other children with water, telling them he was blessing them."[8]

Santos Romero decided that his second-born had accumulated all the knowledge he would need from schoolbooks by age thirteen. Hoping to guide his son into a good trade, he apprenticed young Oscar to one of the best carpenters in town, though it was clear from the beginning that Oscar had other ideas about his future. His siblings remember that as soon as he was released from the carpenter's shop, Oscar went straight to church for his daily prayers. Young Oscar convinced the town mayor to intercede on his behalf and speak of his vocation—both for learning and the priesthood—with his practically-minded father.[9] Santos Romero was eventually persuaded to allow his serious, pious son to leave home for San Miguel—seven hours away on horseback—to study at the minor seminary.

Young Oscar, studious and serious even as a child, would certainly have come of age with a painfully intimate understanding of the plight of El Salvador's subsistence farmers. Bereft of any good, arable land, they competed with large growers to bring a few bushels of coffee or cacao to market or were reduced to complete reliance on the meager wages they could glean from backbreaking work at harvest season.

With such a childhood, Romero surely could viscerally grasp the justice of the land reform campaigns of the 1970s that would provide the spark to El Salvador's civil war. When reformers in El Salvador began to talk of a more equitable distribution of the nation's not insignificant land resources, they described indigenous or mestizo populations seeding or harvesting by a hanging rope. Often the hillsides, the only arable land left for the poor to grow their own subsistence food crops or have an acre or two for market, could only be worked by rope, so steep was their slope. Sixty percent of El Salvador's best land was controlled by less than two percent of its population. The vast majority of the people in this most populous Central American nation was kept in a state of perpetual poverty, bereft of land or gainful employment, trapped in generational cycles of poverty that forced them to remain a perennial resource for the cheap labor needs of the country's tiny class of landholders. It is impossible to exaggerate the wretchedness of the poor in El Salvador. The poor had no land to grow a subsistence crop and often had no place to live at all, relying on day wages to get by.

When coffee became king in El Salvador in the nineteenth century, the industry began to attract European immigrants from Italy, England, and elsewhere in the later part of the century and into the twentieth century. After intermarrying and assimilating with the existing colonial oligarchs, they consolidated into family and economic dynasties of their own. Their thirst for the best lands for growing coffee, on its way to becoming an international commodity of much value, pushed the already marginalized "Ladinos" and indigenous farmers of El Salvador off what little decent land they had left after centuries of oppression from Spanish colonizers. The family dynasties of El Salvador expanded from the original Spanish colonial base to include some of the wealthier and most powerful descendants of the newcomers to El Salvador, who simply seized on the existing colonial order of exploitation and control and shifted it over to the needs of their rising coffee industry. They quickly converted their economic accumulation into political power. That power assured them of control of the rural workforce, crucial to a successful and lucrative annual coffee harvest.

Coffee growers held the presidency in El Salvador from 1898 to 1931 without interruption. Over decades the coffee elite may have ceded direct control of Salvadoran affairs to military dictatorships, but they branched out beyond coffee growing and processing into finance, manufacturing, and tourism until by the time of the civil war, the elites dominated not only the coffee industry, but essentially the rest of the Salvadoran economy.[10]

This social structure created material opulence for a tiny group of Salvadoran families and the deepest deprivation for most other Salvadorans. Essentially all social and economic power was concentrated into the hands of the "catorce," "the 14 families," as the members of the colonial and coffee (or both) dynasties came to be known, a condition that persisted for generations. El Salvador's elite was actually comprised of dozens or more "families," connected by lines of blood, but also by agricultural, political, and commercial interests. "Family" connected Salvadorans could be found in all aspects of the socioeconomic life in El Salvador, and they put those connections in the military and political classes to good use when the perceived interests of the elite were threatened.

These social conditions continued unchanged when a middle-aged Romero was invited into significant positions of influence in the church hierarchy, positions he no doubt achieved because of the relative confidence that he would do little as a church leader to alter El Salvador's social and political landscape.

Few Salvadoran campesinos had the nerve or energy to challenge the rule of the coffee elite. The few who did were subject to ruthless retaliation. How ruthless became clear after a series of what would prove seminal events were set in motion on January 22, 1932, when—responding to a call for general insurrection issued by the Farabundo Martí and the Salvadoran Communist Party—a band of farmers and agricultural laborers revolted in western El Salvador. The farmworkers' revolt was a thing of little consequence and quickly put down. But in a ferocious, punitive campaign that followed the three-day uprising, the Salvadoran National Guard, who ranged in the countryside with complete impunity, engaged in a month-long slaughter of indigenous and Ladino (mixed indigenous and Hispanic) communities that came to be known as the *matanza* (the massacre).

Understanding the events and implications of the *matanza* is important because it helps explain what at first glance appears to be incomprehensible brutality leading up to and including the assassination of Oscar Romero and all the unspeakable violence that followed in the next twelve years of civil war in El Salvador. During the initial insurrection of the indigenous and Ladino farmworkers, who had armed themselves with machetes and farm tools, the estates of a number of Salvadoran planters had been attacked. The threat of a final accounting for the long-suffering of the indigenous and mestizo communities of El Salvador is a dark constant in the psyche of El Salvador's ruling families. This campesino uprising was that dark dread made real, even as it remained largely ineffective in its own right.

Panicked landowners and their surrogates joined the National Guard in a vast bloodletting that seemed aimed at assuaging to the most horrific degree imaginable this terror of retribution. Anyone who looked "like an indian" or a campesino was assumed to be part of the uprising and was killed. Mass graves overflowed; drainage ditches were filled with bodies, fed on by pigs, dogs, and vultures. The scale of the slaughter is unknowable, but the killings decades later during the civil war—bodies piling up on garbage heaps and victims treated with the most unspeakable tortures—were an eerie echo of the bloody mayhem of the *matanza*. The initial three-day uprising in January claimed the lives of perhaps twenty to thirty. By the end of the month of the *matanza*, as many as twenty-five to thirty thousand campesinos and their families had been killed, perhaps as much as two percent of the Salvadoran population in 1932.[11]

The event scorched the national psyche. In the retelling of the ruling elite, still in force at the time of the murder of the archbishop, the event came to be mythologized as a fight between the forces of reason and progress against a swirling horde of primitive rage and violence. According to this story, the victims of the *matanza* were located not among the campesinos and indigenous but among the middle and land-owning classes who had joined the heroic National Guard in turning back a barbarian assault on civilization. It was a false, inverted reflection of the true *matanza*, but it was deeply powerful.

This illusory memory of the *matanza* still influenced the imagination and ideology of the elite by the time social tensions again were reaching explosive force when Romero became archbishop. It also directly guided their overwrought assessment of the threat from church-influenced demands for social reforms and the brutal strategy of murder and suppression the national elite opted to accept to put down this latest uprising. Faced with catechists seeking to spread liberation among the campesinos in the countryside and the dislocated poor in the cities and social reformers demanding social justice and land reform, the elite saw again a vicious, mindless horde on the rise and responded accordingly.

How does one become a murderer of one's own people? How does a nation's military become the agent of so vast a bloodletting of the men, women, and children it has sworn to defend and protect? Many of the young men who served in the Salvadoran military had backgrounds and life experiences little different from the campesinos and city dwellers they were commanded to kill. Many were surely reluctant combatants and participants in state-sponsored violence against the Salvadoran people.

Even one of the men who was part of the operation to murder the archbishop (having been enlisted to drive a car while visiting the conspirators to buy cocaine) swears he would have killed the leaders of the assassination with his own hands if he knew they were planning to kill the archbishop.

Long before the murder of Romero, the coconspirators of his killing among the wealthy and the manipulators of opinion, the owners of right-wing media outlets, laid the seeds for the seething anger and resentment toward the Catholic clergy in general and the archbishop specifically. Tensions were brewing in El Salvador for years as the rapidly expanding coffee market created an export boom that led to emerging techniques in coffee and other export crop agricultural production that reduced labor requirements but meant a growing appetite for "unproductive" land typically held by rural, subsistence tenant farmers. The reduced labor force expectations and loss of farmland meant a vast dislocation of rural Salvadorans, who took refuge in the nation's cities in search of food, shelter, and work.

This became a restive "pobretariado," not a proletariat, but literally a "poorletariat" that eventually raised anxieties among El Salvador's military and economic elites.[12] Had the elite responded to this economic and social crisis with housing, training, or better educational opportunities instead of transferring a rural repression into an urban environment, the story of El Salvador in the 1980s would no doubt have ended less tragically.

The "poorletariat" turned to the church for physical and spiritual succor during this difficult time. From their catechists and clerics, sometimes even from their prelates, they heard a message of spiritual liberation that was grounded in a release from their material suffering. Some, hearing that message and after enduring all they could from the intractable status quo, found their way to "Marx through Jesus Christ," as sociologist Jeffrey Paige put it.[13] Others joined the church in seeking a peaceful course toward social justice.

To the ruling oligarchs of El Salvador, either path meant a death sentence and increasingly it meant the church itself was beginning to be perceived as an enemy of the state and the social order. In 1977 and 1978 fifteen priests and lay leaders were murdered as the liberation preached by the church began to be interpreted not as a message of redemption and community and mutual sacrifice, but as a political call to revolution. To El Salvador's oligarchs, with the haunting events of the 1932 *matanza* a searing, collective memory, Christianity as much as Marxism, the Eucharist as much as revolution, became an existential threat that had to be ruthlessly put down. The murder of Romero was a simple demonstration of how far it was willing to go to protect its status and privilege.

CHAPTER THREE

The Young Priest

As the 1932 *matanza* peaked, young Oscar was continuing his studies at the minor seminary in San Miguel under the direction of the Claretian Missionaries, which he had entered at thirteen. Biographer Jesús Delgado located a poem Romero wrote then, turning over this teenager's understanding of what it meant to be a priest:

> Your word is pardon and gentleness for the penitent,
> your word is holy instruction, eternal teaching;
> it is light to brighten, advice to hearten;
> it is voice of hope, fire that burns,
> way, truth, sublime splendor,
> life . . . eternity . . .
> But not is the temple alone your battlefield;
> you range the world with your sword upraised,
> the redeeming cross.
> And cannon's roar daunts you not;
> nor does clash of steel when
> you hear the church's voice
> call to you earnestly with plaintive voice,
> for cruel men with cruel blades
> have wounded her to the point of death.[1]

Another biographer, James Brockman, SJ, reviewing the poem, describes Romero "looking forward to the priesthood idealistically, somewhat romantically."[2] And that's true enough, but reading these teenager's words now and knowing what was to come, it is hard not to note a tragic foreshadowing in the verse. If indeed he held a romantic view of the priesthood, it was one he maintained to the end, one from which he was apparently able to draw much strength and solace.

He continued his studies at the national seminary, now being instructed by the Jesuits. He finished his studies at the Jesuits' Gregorian Institute in Rome, where he spent the war years (1939–43) far from El Salvador, an often cold, hungry, and poor seminarian, enduring the deprivations of the war alongside the Italian people. He came to admire Pius XI because of his principled stand against Nazism and Fascism.[3] He was ordained in Rome in 1942; his family was unable to attend because of wartime travel restrictions.

Brockman writes that a more mature view of the priesthood appears in some words that the twenty-two-year-old Romero wrote when he was a seminarian in Rome, published in the students' magazine of the Latin American College in March of 1940: "This is your heritage, O priest: the cross. And this is your mission: to portion out the cross. Bearer of pardon and peace, the priest runs to the bed of the dying, and a cross in his hand is the key that opens the heavens and closes the abyss."[4]

In 1943 Romero was called home early, before he finished his doctorate, owing to an acute need for priests in El Salvador. The serious, pious child had grown into a serious, pious priest. After a brief assignment as pastor in Anamorós, a Salvadoran mountain town much like Ciudad Barrios where he grew up, Romero was called back to the provincial capital San Miguel to be secretary of the diocese, a job he would hold for the next twenty-three years. It was not his only role in San Miguel; he also was pastor of the cathedral parish and chaplain at another. He was an assistant editor, then the editor of the diocesan paper. Romero was an energetic "doer" in San Miguel, assuming pastoral odd jobs as they materialized, including oversight of the completion of the cathedral. His reputation as a preacher grew, and before long his sermons were carried live by five of the small city's radio stations.[5]

In San Miguel, he was indefatigable, visiting the country-side and the county jail, promoting any number of devotional and self-help groups within the diocese, including the Legion of Mary, Alcoholics Anonymous, Catholic Action, and Cursillos de Cristiandad. He saw to it that the local Caritas not only distributed food among the poor, but also taught the people about nutrition. "He was always concerned with the whole person's welfare," a woman who worked with him then remarked. A dear friend, Salvador Barraza, remembered that in preaching he insisted on expressing a religion that dealt with daily life, not mere piety.[6]

Father Romero was overly bothered by the liberties other priests sometimes took. Going about in public without wearing their cassocks was the kind of minor annoyance that the young priest allowed to get the better of him, eventually working himself into a permanent boil over this lack of fidelity to clerical appearances.[7] Worse, some of the priests of San Miguel were occasionally caught drinking and consorting with prostitutes.

A scolding scrupulousness would be a problem throughout his career. It would eventually generate animus with whole generations of priests when later in life as an auxiliary bishop he made it his business to police doctrinal fidelity with the same vigor he attached to sartorial inspections.

Fortunately his scrupulousness extended to his duties as pastor. Romero denied no one, to the point of his own physical exhaustion. Most of the community's poorest, those without any land to call their own, huddled together in huts of board and tin on lifeless fields of volcanic rock known as "La Curruncha." The community's reputation was fierce (a den of thieves, it was said) and its conditions were deplorable: ice cold at night and scorching under the midday sun. Yet at any hour of the day or night Romero was ready to respond to a call for a blessing or extreme unction even among these most forlorn of San Miguel society. "It was always the same thing," a sister who had worked with the poor of La Curruncha recalled. When death approached and the poor were asked, "Do you want some medicine?" without fail, it was: "We want to speak with Father Romero."

"And he never told them no."[8]

In San Miguel, Father Romero began what would be another lifelong habit, that of maintaining a close relationship to the rich and the powerful in his community. To his critics the nurturing of such friendships and connections spoke to a certain vanity and credulity in Romero. Later in life, when social proximity to the elite of El Salvador seemed a statement of complicity with the oppression of Salvadoran campesinos, Romero's associations with the powerful took a much more sinister tone. In the eyes of many they would mark him as an enemy of progress and justice within both the church and Salvadoran society.

But for his many acquaintances and friendships among the rich and connected, Romero also maintained rich relationships with the working class and the downtrodden. His closest friend in life, Salvador Barraza, was not exactly poor, but as a shoe merchant was hardly among the Salvadoran elite.

Romero was especially regarded as a soft touch by the alcoholics of San Miguel, maybe because his own brother Gustavo had struggled with alcoholism. Perhaps it was Gustavo's face he saw when a handout was requested. Each morning around the wall of the church, the town's alcohol-ics, its panhandlers, and even its prostitutes lined to wait for a little *moneda* from him because Father never said no, and he always kept a few *colónes* in his pockets. Romero housed alcoholics and homeless old people in the church convent and paid bus fare for the campesinos returning to the countryside. He even protected the town's shoeshine boys and organized them into a self-help collective. One resident of San Miguel remembered that Romero was "like St. Vincent de Paul—a mass of poor people always followed him around."[9]

Such associations came naturally to Romero. Until almost the end of his life, his personal theology and spirituality remained resolutely old-fashioned. Certainly he had an obli-gation to materially help the needy of San Miguel, and he did, but his responsibility also extended to the more difficult challenge of saving souls among the rich and comfortable of San Miguel. There weren't many of them, and Father Romero had little difficulty establishing personal contact with most, if not all.

His dual role—a pastor to serve the poor and save the rich—was united through these relationships. Couldn't he after all persuade the rich to help him serve the poor of San Miguel and in this way prod them along further toward salvation? This vision of Christian community left little room for Marxist critiques of economic systems of oppres-sion. It was focused firmly on old-fashioned conceits about how the spiritual world—and ultimately salvation—was supposed to operate. The poor suffered, surely, but they should do so with as little complaint and conflict as they could offer up in recompense. Their reward would be great for fortitude in this life. And the rich that Romero could reach, those willing to help with timely donations to assist the poor, surely those temporal offerings would assist them through the eye of the needle when their time came as well.

Romero had become close to San Miguel's coffee plantation owners. He broke bread with them on their farms, he collected their donations for the poor, and he would celebrate special masses for them in their homes. At Christmas he would join them in distributing gifts to the poor whose hard labor kept their plantations afloat.

But he was no mere puppet of the rich as was presumed years later by the radical priests who would watch his installation as archbishop in barely disguised scorn and despair.

Some of the fine women of San Miguel got the idea that Romero's simple, even shabby, room at the rectory was an embarrassment. They conspired to fix up the room with a fine bed, linens, and elegant curtains when Romero was away. But when he returned Father Romero was furious to discover the transformation and gave everything away to people passing in the street, restoring his simple cot and old chair and fuming about the manipulative impulses of the wealthy.[10] It was fine for him to collect money for the poor from them, but Romero personally would not be bought off so cheaply.

In San Miguel Father Romero also began his career as a communicator. The young priest was happy to take advantage of the most modern medium of his time, the radio, in order to effect his ministry. (El Salvador's minor seminary had been run by the Claretians, a Spanish order well-known for its interest in using the technology and communication tools of the times for the work of evangelization. Perhaps the Claretians can claim a little credit for his success as a communicator.) Throughout his career Romero would show a keen interest in using mass communication to reach the faithful and those on the verge of being so. He made good use of newspapers and radio broadcasts to reach his flock. His enthusiasm for radio communication would prove crucial to the role he would play supporting the campesinos of El Salvador and as archbishop bringing attention to their plight. In El Salvador the regular media was more or less bought and paid for by the ruling elite. Romero's weekly homily, broadcast live over the radio, was all the unadulterated news that many were able to hear.

On Radio Chaparrastique, named for the region's looming volcano, Romero became a well-known personality because of his morning and evening prayer programs. Years later he would perform the role of recounting to Salvadorans the terrible news of the day that the nation's national press refused to broadcast. On Radio Chaparrastique, Romero enthralled his audience with stories and letters told out of real life, sent in to him by the people themselves, such as questions about catechism and requests for alms or advice.

A new bishop in 1968 meant the end of an era for San Miguel and for Monseñor Oscar Romero. An American Franciscan, Bishop Lawrence Graziano, had been appointed over Romero's head, and this US missionary was not as willing as his predecessor had been to allow Romero to monopolize so many diocesan roles and assume so much responsibility. Graziano was also aware of the tensions that had developed between Romero and many of the priests of the diocese because of the various scoldings they had endured courtesy of diocese's de facto disciplinarian and fallback factotum.[11] San Miguel's outgoing Bishop Miguel Machado had been better known for offering loans at extortionists' rates than sound guidance or support for his pastors, and Romero had stepped in to fill the void.[12] Many had believed Romero was intended to become San Miguel's next bishop. Instead he was named secretary general of the national bishops' conference and in September 1967 was on his way to San Salvador.

Some in the diocese believed Father Romero must have been bitter to be passed over, but physical and emotional exhaustion better characterized his condition when he left San Miguel. In 1966 Romero had been diagnosed psychologically with obsessive-compulsive personality disorder and spiritually with "scrupulosity," a psychic tag team that rendered him a near physical and mental wreck by the time his tenure in San Miguel had ended. He had accomplished much within the diocese and had become renowned for his many successes. The omnipresent cleric had also made an impression because of his preaching, the breadth of the spiritual and practical responsibilities he had assumed in San Miguel, and the many accomplishments he had made in the diocese. But privately, as a man approaching middle age, he was spent, struggling with a loss of confidence, a sense of personal failure, and a deep loneliness. It seems his time as the diocesan scold had greatly built up his sense of isolation. He keenly felt the need for friendship and support from his fellow priests and relationships with other people even as he drove them, out of a sense of acute attentiveness to his position—his scrupulosity—further away.

Romero may have been relieved to accept an introvert's role as secretary to the bishops' conference after his exhausting duties in San Miguel. Unfortunately his timing was epically poor. In 1967 the doors and windows of the global church had been blown open by Vatican II; there were times the church seemed to be reeling before a gale of transformation. Romero's job was to make sense of the documents of Vatican II—and soon thereafter the even more startling statements emerging from Medellín—and craft the response of the Salvadoran bishops. His scrupulosity would serve him well in this enterprise. Despite his unease with what he was reading, Romero was carefully studying the documents, subconsciously building a foundation for a superior insight into their message and appreciation for the direction the church should be taking.

Romero would be alternately guided and troubled by a few revolutionary church documents. Several pastoral statements that he penned himself were efforts to explain the perilous path he felt compelled to take for himself and the church in El Salvador.

Like the dutiful, conscientious prelate he was, he carefully studied the documents of Vatican II in an effort to understand what the council meant for him and his beloved church. For years he was deeply troubled by the implications of Vatican II, but that fear and trembling were nothing compared to the agitation that another document, this one prepared by his fellow bishops, would arouse in him.

Imbued with the spirit of the council, the bishops of Latin America had met in Medellín, Colombia, in 1967. When they departed and issued the meeting's "Medellín documents," the church in Latin America, indeed all over the world, would never quite be the same. Among other tradition-breaking discussions, Medellín was the first church document to officially speak of a social teaching ethic that came to be defined as the "preferential option for the poor." The concept was a part of a broad indictment of the vast inequities of life in Latin America and the church's passive or direct role in maintaining them.

"Pure fear" was how an acquaintance of Romero described his reaction to Medellín. A Jesuit teaching at the seminary described running into a speechless Romero "as if the wind had been knocked out of him," as he considered the Medellín statement, terrified of the "new" that it represented. "Monseñor, your problem is you don't have enough faith," the Jesuit told him.[13]

Romero, who would choose the episcopal motto "Sentir con la Iglesia" (to be of one mind with the church), could not ignore the revolutionary earthquake of Vatican II and the resulting aftershock of Medellín. As much as the new thinking terrified him—one priest recalled that Romero experienced a noticeable facial tic, a twitching lower lip, at the mere mention of Medellín—he remained always the dutiful seminarian. He refused, as some fellow Salvadoran bishops did, to renounce or ignore Medellín, but continued to read and pray over its documents and the new teaching that was emerging from Vatican II. He indeed wanted to be one with the church, and he steeled himself to understand what that meant in the church's—and El Salvador's—contemporary milieu.

Medellín proclaimed: "Let there be seen in Latin America the ever brighter face of a church authentically poor, missionary, and paschal, disentangled from all temporal power, and daringly committed to the freedom of the whole person and of all persons."[14] Romero struggled to understand how to accept and to practically enliven Medellín. It was not until the killing of Rutilio Grande, however, that it can be said the word of Medellín came to life for him. Medellín had been the source of agony, now it would become a blueprint for leading the church through its "paschal hour."

Though he had literally taken Vatican II's message of renewal to heart and used its spirit of reopening and restoration to guide a period of personal reflection and renewal, Romero remained uncomfortable with the loosening of clerical prohibitions and changing of what had been static, dependable roles and protocols that he was observing his fellow priests accepting, even initiating. During his time as secretary general of the Salvadoran bishops' conference (and later as auxiliary bishop), Monseñor Romero would play the role of culture warrior for the old guard, taking to the barricades of the diocesan newspaper *Orientación* in regular confrontations with young priests who were moving past both clerical traditions and expectations and pushing the church forward into a confrontation with the Salvadoran status quo.[15]

His ordination in June 1970 as auxiliary bishop of San Salvador was an epic affair and the source of minor scandal, given the new direction the church seemed to be taking in its preferential option for the poor and the clerical asceticism proposed by Medellín just a few years earlier. While the priests of the diocese were growing in their dismay at the poverty of the people and facing intimidation and increasingly rough treatment from Salvadoran security forces, Romero's elaborate ordination as bishop seemed an unwelcome throwback to times these future-minded priests were attempting to move beyond. The affair was primed with busloads of admirers and friends delivered to San Salvador from San Miguel just for the celebration. All the bishops of El Salvador attended, of course, but the grand event also drew the papal nuncio and a retrograde figure much loathed among the progressive priests of El Salvador, Cardinal Mario Casriego of Guatemala. (Casriego was not exactly simpatico to progressive priests in his own country. He denied that priests were being hunted down in Guatemala—they were—and memorably suggested: "If you mix in politics, you get what you deserve.") President Fidel Sánchez Hernández was there, along with a score of local political figures and faces from the business and landholding classes. How much of the episcopal overkill can be laid at Romero's feet is not clear. His friends from San Miguel, especially Salvador Barraza, claim much of the credit for arranging the celebration, and as master of ceremonies Rutilio Grande devoted weeks to preparing the liturgy itself.

A famous photo captures Romero blessing the assembled, escorted by Grande and accompanied by the prelate he would in a few years replace in San Salvador, Archbishop Luis Chávez y González (no stranger himself to the scorn of his brother bishops because of his "radical" innovations). The event represented a climax of sorts for the episcopal old guard of El Salvador, a fleeting remembrance of past ordinations before the nation's coming political storm and the arrival of a new clerical style. The ostentatious ordination represented a final display, at least for many years after Romero's martyrdom, of episcopal privilege many believed was being washed away by Vatican II, Medellín, and later the bishops' conference in Puebla, Mexico.

As defender of the church against its young turks, Romero had his work cut out for him. The day following his ordination, the national pastoral week in El Salvador began and the winds of Vatican II and especially Medellín began to move strongly through the streets of the capital. The event, ignored or boycotted by some of El Salvador's rural bishops, was organized and endorsed by the archbishop of San Salvador Chavéz and his auxiliary bishop Arturo Rivera. It was a pivotal moment for the priests and active laypeople of the archdiocese and set the agenda for the beginning of greater lay involvement and the foundation for Christian base communities that were already beginning to emerge in the countryside.

These twin developments, which filled so many with enthusiasm and hope, would come in the end to be the source of much heartache and suffering in El Salvador. Many of the catechists became community leaders and organizers who came to be perceived, targeted, and finally liquidated as subversives and communists by the Salvadoran elite through their agents in the security forces. The essential and new understanding promulgated by Medellín and the new thinking that would eventually coalesce into liberation theology—that God does not "will" social injustice, that, in fact, on the contrary Christians are actively called to confront matters of social inequity and discrimination—represented an immediate and, to the thinking of many Salvadoran elite, an existential challenge to the order that had delivered to them so much material comfort and social prestige.

The psychic lesion of the *matanza* left El Salvador's landholders and business class trapped in an either-or, black-and-white thinking. For others to have something meant they would have nothing or worse than nothing; the long-feared indigenous retribution that would mean a bloody annihilation of the landholding class. Few could appreciate the possibility of a third way, including Romero, who would one day come to embody that alternative, nonviolent path to justice and social rapprochement. Then Romero's idea of harmony was grounded in his past experiences as mediator between rich and poor, a mendicant before the rich on behalf of the poor and to the poor a consoler and confidante, guiding them through a sorrowful acceptance of their plight in life with an eye always on the divine reward and justice that awaited all.

Romero was part of a commission charged with reviewing the conclusions of the pastoral week and revising it so that its more radical-sounding elements might be toned down to a degree acceptable to El Salvador's worried conservative prelates. It was the beginning of such an intercessory role that he would play as an auxiliary bishop.

His true redoubt against the "radical" clerics of El Salvador, however, was *Orientación*. Already a regular contributor, as auxiliary bishop he became the diocesan paper's editor. From its pages he was able to fire broadsides at those priests whose indifference to clerical cassocks was only the beginning of ecclesial malfeasance. Some were observed becoming overly familiar with laypeople, especially those of the opposite sex, even surrendering some pastoral authority to them. But worst of all were the presumed closet Marxists among them. It did not take much to be so labeled.

Two Jesuits, for instance, led some spiritual exercises with the clergy of San Salvador at the request of Archbishop Chávez. The discussion broke down over the role of the contemporary priest in the political order of the times. Romero stealthily observed from the back of the meeting room without adding a word to the difficult conversation. Two weeks later he blasted the Jesuits by name in *Orientación*, complaining that their version of spiritual exercises contained little content that was spiritual, but was well-reinforced with political sociology—Marxist political sociology to boot! Furious, one of the Jesuits wrote a lengthy rebuttal arguing that such accusations were precisely the kind of rhetoric that put lives in jeopardy even as properly enlightened priests were trying to make real the changes envisioned in Medellín and Vatican II. To that Jesuit's surprise, Romero published the entire rejoinder, but made sure he reserved the editorial last word for himself: He stood by his judgment, and he could still prove they were Marxists. "Nobody could beat him at being stubborn," the Jesuit remembered.[16]

By the elections of 1972 not even an obstinate Romero could pretend that the old ways were enough to suffice within the swirling tensions of contemporary El Salvador. UNO, the Unión Nacional Opositora, a coalition of Christian and Social Democrats that included El Salvador's tiny Communist Party, created an unprecedented challenge to the PCN, the Partido de Conciliación Nacional, the "eternal party of the military." The Salvadoran people came out in massive support of UNO, determined to make the most of this unprecedented opportunity for real and peaceful democratic change after decades of oligarchic rule. The people voted; the outcome was another blatant fraud. Colonel Arturo Armando Molina (his son Mario Molina would be implicated as one of the conspirators in Romero's assassination) was "elected" the new president of El Salvador, continuing a forty-year stretch of essentially uninterrupted military-connected authoritarian rule.

Worse than the election fraud, however, was the aftermath. On March 25, protestors gathered in San Salvador. The government declared a state of siege and martial law throughout El Salvador in a response calculated to suppress any resistance to the new president. Some progressive members of the military took matters into their own hands and launched an ill-conceived and executed attempted coup, reluctantly supported by the losing candidate Napoleon Duarte. After the coup was put down, Duarte, politically beaten by the machinations of the elite and literally beaten by Salvadoran military after he was dragged out of diplomatic sanctuary, was allowed to leave El Salvador for exile in Venezuela. On Holy Thursday night in El Carmen, a village of Romero's old diocese San Miguel, the army materialized and collected half a dozen campesinos from their homes. The men went missing for several days as relatives searched in vain. On Holy Saturday the mystery ended as the military returned and dumped their tortured, lifeless bodies on the road into El Carmen.

The following Monday Father Miguel Ventura went to see the bishop of San Miguel, Eduardo Álvarez, to discuss how he wanted to respond. Bishop Álvarez was also a colonel in the Salvadoran army. Asked by Ventura if he wanted to go to El Carmen to console the people because "they need it," he replied, "They need it?! Ha! Those people were asking for it. Now they'll just have to take what's coming to them!"

Stunned and increasingly troubled, Father Ventura took the matter to Romero in San Salvador, and though the new auxiliary bishop was plainly upset by what he heard—and what he heard of Bishop Álvarez's response—he told Ventura that it wouldn't be "prudent" for him to travel to El Carmen and stand with the people there. He ineffectually urged Ventura to take the matter to the papal nuncio, a close friend of the recently "elected" President Molina.[17]

That empathy checked by cautiousness would typify the tone and content of Romero's episcopal response to the rapidly-changing social conditions and events he was forced to confront. In July 1972 Romero joined other Salvadoran bishops supporting President Molina's decision to occupy the national university. Hundreds were arrested and beaten by Salvadoran military, and the university would be closed for a year. This direct intervention by the bishops in the events of the day (they denounced "subversive" elements at work within the university) is worth noting. Unlike other gestures that Romero in a few years' time would make on behalf of those struggling for political reform and social justice, the bishops' statement in this instance was not denounced as a political intrusion by the church in matters it had no business attending to.

For his part during this period, Romero attended to a one-man struggle with "subversives" within the church in his newspaper columns and commentary for radio and television. Invited to join some of the people he was criticizing for Mass in Zacamil, a community near the capital, he was confronted by three hundred or so members of El Salvador's base communities who quickly admonished the astonished bishop because of some of his public positions against the pastoral initiatives to which they had dedicated themselves. Romero was armed with "briefcases full of texts" of various South American bishops denouncing the base communities' movement; the priests and catechists were armed with the documents of Vatican II and Medellín. Some of those at the "Mass" (the event was quickly disintegrating into a shouting match) had been among those beaten at the university.

The more Romero insisted that he had proof that subversion was afoot at the university, the more exasperated the laypeople and priests became. A furious Romero finally shouted before storming off, "You're not doing pastoral work here at all! You're doing political work! And you haven't called me to a Mass! You've called me to a meeting of subversives!"[18] Though this kind of public breakdown was unusual, it typified Romero's years of struggle and suspicion with the practical implications of the church's quickly evolving understanding of its role in socioeconomic flash points like El Salvador.

It was hardly his only confrontation with "progressive" forces during this period. As auxiliary, Romero became the main protagonist in two memorable campaigns against "progressive" priests in El Salvador. Romero became involved in a particularly bruising campaign to evict the Jesuits from the national seminary, despite his long association with the order and his regular personal practice of Ignatian spirituality. The instructors were accused of preaching politics, not Jesus, to Salvadoran seminarians. He was among the primary objectors to the discourse encouraged by the national seminary's Jesuit directors, though the Jesuits had been running the seminary for decades (and he in fact at the time was living— uncomfortably—among them at the seminary). Romero became one of the bishops who forced the order out of the seminary, promoting rumors of Marxist indoctrination and sexual dalliances with loose women within the seminary, even the idea that communist "bomb making" was being orchestrated within its study halls. Romero's public and private campaign would eventually succeed—something he would come to feel ashamed of in just a few short years. Having guided the seminary for five decades, the Jesuits were expelled in 1972. Romero himself was appointed rector and the seminary was reopened with new faculty and new seminarians, presumably untainted by Jesuit instruction. With few students and with costs mounting, the bishops decided to close the seminary completely just a half year later, the entire fiasco ultimately representing an embarrassment for the hectoring auxiliary bishop Romero.[19]

This first skirmish with the Jesuits was a prelude to another campaign to force them out of a San Salvador high school. Central American Jesuits had replaced Spanish Jesuits in command of the school and its direction. The new Jesuits at the high school, Externado San José, had added evening and weekend classes intended for the poor children from San Salvador's barrios; they began to offer instruction in sociology to the children of the elite who attended the school and even took them on field trips outside the confines of the school and into the barrios of the poor nearby. The tensions with the church of the past and its not-so-subtle alignment with the ruling elite, and whatever form the church of the future would take in determining what a preferential option for the poor actually meant, were becoming acute, and to many, alarming. Certainly alarmed were a few of the parents of these Jesuit-educated students, who were unhappy about the penetrating questions suddenly being asked by their children around the dinner table and were not shy about complaining to their connection in the archdiocese, Bishop Romero. In an editorial in *Orientación*, Romero lashed out at this "falsely liberating education" now offered by the renegade Jesuits and the alleged disdain with which they treated their predecessors. He denounced the "demagogy and Marxism" that could be found among "pamphlets and literature" handed out at the school "of known red origin." The editorial started an uproar that lasted for months and was only ended after Archbishop Chavéz heard a report that exonerated the school by a commission he had established to investigate the charges.

Though he did not succeed in forcing them out of the high school, the two episodes—and his enthusiastic participation in both—go a long way to explaining why Romero's appointment to archbishop in 1977 was greeted with such dismay by El Salvador's Jesuit priests and like-minded clerics around the country and with hosannas within the homes of more socially complacent Salvadorans.

Ironically, while publicly campaigning against the Jesuits, Romero was engaged in a silent, personal struggle with his own psychological demons and leaned heavily for spiritual support on Ignatian practices. He was well aware of his problems with perfectionism, his desperate need for relationship and support with his fellow priests, and perverse impulses that thwarted any progress toward making those connections. The Ignatian practice of the daily examen helped him through this internal crisis. Despite the rigid public posture he believed he had no choice but to maintain, in the quiet of his nightly rituals of prayer and meditation, Romero longed to live as a real pastor, not as an insufferable bureaucrat; he longed to serve and live a life engaged with the people. The "conversion" he would experience in 1977 may have first taken root in these yearning examens.

Romero's spiritual development owed something to Claretian piety and evangelical zeal learned in minor seminary, the deep introspection and self-examination inculcated at various points of his life from the Jesuits, and the austere discipline, always a personal trait, but reinforced by his exposure late in life to spiritual counseling from members of Opus Dei. On top of this complex of Catholic spiritual traditions, Romero himself, responding to his intermittent bouts of anxiety and depression, sought out psychoanalysis as a means to better understand the emotional and psychological currents that drove him. Many marveled at Romero's ability to adapt to the new conditions he confronted as archbishop, especially since so late in his life one might expect Romero to have become more brittle in his outlook. Ironically it may have been his desire to better understand his inflexibility and at times crippling scrupulousness that allowed this middle-aged man to reestablish such personal and sociological flexibility through prayer, introspection, and analysis.

Romero's experience with psychoanalysis allowed him to better understand the behaviors that were propelling his loneliness, and in typical fashion he responded with lists of personal reforms meant to allow him to experience more intimate—but, of course, not too intimate—relationships with laypeople and with his fellow priests. The anxious tendencies he combated drove him into a conservative funk for years, clinging to the old ways and unwilling to accept the evolving post-Vatican II clerical reality. Oddly enough his issue with scrupulousness offered an opening to the conversion that the progressive priests would one day celebrate in this prelate all had presumed was a hopeless ecclesial neanderthal.

CHAPTER FOUR

The Cautious Cleric

As auxiliary bishop, Romero's campaign against recalci-
trant clerics in San Salvador would be short-lived. Events
in El Salvador were galloping past all old understandings
of the church. However traditional Romero's perception of
the role of the church in the lived reality of the people may
have been, he was still a man of the people, a man who had
come from the people and cared for the people. Despite the
grim authoritarianism he displayed in public, he yearned to
perform a more pastoral service with and for the people,
and he longed for the respect and comradeship of his fellow
priests. He had never been indifferent to the suffering of the
people even though he was perplexed by the changing political and ecclesial milieus he inhabited. His transformation
was beginning though he did not know it himself. It would
not take much for the heroic Romero, who would become
beloved of the people of El Salvador and soon all over the
world, to emerge from this humorless clerical cocoon.

Monseñor Romero's grim tour of duty as auxiliary in San
Salvador endured a final kerfuffle in 1974. Selected to serve
as El Salvador's delegate to the bishops' synod in Rome,

Romero, mentally scattered and physically spent because of his many responsibilities, declined the honor. When the bishops decided that his partner auxiliary Rivera should go in his stead, Romero reconsidered his perhaps too-hasty decision, concerned that Rivera was too radical in his views to represent the Salvadoran bishops, and attempted to push Rivera out of the duty. Rivera recalled that Romero made little effort to conceal the doubts he held about his fellow auxiliary. To him Romero seemed to be going through a period of depression at the time and "looked exhausted." Once again, unable to delegate responsibilities to others and dissatisfied with the work he perceived subordinates capable of performing, he had overtasked himself.[1]

Before more hard feelings could have been generated by the incident, Romero was named to lead the diocese of Santiago de María. To Romero, the honor was a vindication of his *lucha* with the forces of change in El Salvador and an endorsement of the cautious interpretation of the spirit of Vatican II that he had followed.[2] In a parting shot editorial in *Orientación*, Romero noted his "regret" for the "explicitly worldly, violent, and uncontrolled conduct of those who have tried to make use of religion to destroy the spiritual base of religion."

"In the name of faith," he wrote, "those who have lost their faith have tried to struggle against the faith," but "for our part, we have preferred to adhere to that which is certain, to cling with fear and trembling to the rock of Peter . . . instead of leaping like reckless and foolhardy acrobats to the speculations of the impudent thinkers of social movements of dubious origin . . ."

Recharged by his appointment to Santiago de María, Romero added, "This trust of the pope in its editor must also be interpreted as the most solemn backing of the church's magisterium for the ideology that has inspired the paper's pages under this editorship," constituting a "silent approval" that "determines the route to follow."

It would not be a route Romero followed for long. In Santiago Romero would come face-to-face with the reality that he, like many clerics of his era and position in El Salvador, had hidden from within archdiocesan offices and bureaucratic duties. In Santiago the conflict between the haves and the have-nothings of Salvadoran society was out in the open, literally, in the streets where the itinerant, landless coffee harvesters or cotton pickers "lived," exposed to the cold or predators that accompanied Santiago's nights. Their vulnerability and powerlessness was complete, and it was sometimes fatal.

Romero soon became embroiled in the kind of bureaucratic and ideological battles he had joined in San Salvador. Like his efforts to shut down disquieting instruction by the Jesuits in San Salvador, the new bishop of Santiago de María struggled over a response to Los Naranjos, a learning and training center for campesinos that was offering catechetical development and classes in literacy, but also a "National Reality" curriculum. This curriculum attempted to teach the diocese's campesinos about the political context of their times: how their once communal lands had been taken away during the nineteenth and early twentieth centuries and how land reform might begin to respond to that injustice. After hearing complaints about the subversive instruction taking place at Los Naranjos, Romero sat in a National Reality class himself, listening to a priest offering a history of land ownership and the need for agrarian reform.

He later decided that the classes themselves might not be heresy, but they were certainly unwise. He explained to one of the priests running the program that he worried about the people in the program, simple campesinos, and what the result of their education might be. He did not try to deny the justice or accuracy of the teaching within the classes, just that "we don't know what kinds of things they're going to say when they go back to their villages, because we lose control over them . . ."[3]

On July 30, 1975, troops in San Salvador gunned down some forty students protesting the government's closing of the university at Santa Ana. The incident provoked horror and outrage around the country and demonstrations in the capital. After a priest from the center joined a group occupying the San Salvador cathedral in protest of the killing of the students, Romero's mind was made up. This time no coordinated media campaign was required. As the bishop of Santiago de María, Romero simply ordered the center closed.[4] He eventually had the more provocative components of the center's curriculum toned down and the instruction itself was reorganized so that it could be parish-based and more easily supervised by local priests, but the closure raised Romero's esteem in the eyes of the papal nuncio Emanuele Gerada, and it would be remembered when the nuncio was called upon to make his recommendations to Rome for a replacement to Archbishop Chávez.[5]

Romero was soon to be tutored directly in the "national reality." Like the rest of El Salvador, gross inequities in land ownership were maintained in his new diocese. Absentee landowners drove the poor off the most arable earth, whether they used it or not, and many did not even offer migrant laborers any sort of shelter during harvest season, driving most of the poor to live along the sides of the region's roads. Worse, the landless laborers were often cheated out of the abysmal pay they were offered.

Journalist Phillip Berryman, using the pseudonym Edmundo Moran to disguise his identity (writing about El Salvador while regularly visiting it was not a safe proposition at the time), in *America* magazine in 1978 described

the signs of Romero's times, the economic landscape of El
Salvador. Land and wealth were concentrated into the hands
of a few, and the country's agricultural production was ori-
ented to export "and profits for a few."

"Ever more peasants are landless," Berryman said. "In
1961, the number was only 30,000, while today it is 266,000.
Today [1977], money buys only 38 percent of the beans,
corn, salt, sugar and other necessities that it bought in 1972,
but the minimum wage for a day's agricultural work has
risen only from $1.28 to $2.40 during that time. This year,
inflation is estimated at 22 percent, but there is no minimum-
wage increase for cotton and sugar harvesters."[6] As much as
seventy-five percent of the children of El Salvador were mal-
nourished; infant mortality exceeded sixty percent.

Berryman describes a social construct that depicts what
Medellín had called "institutionalized violence," whereby
the nature of the state, the economy, or the resulting social
structures—a permeating, unconscious reality—does harm
to the many in the service of the few. It was these conditions
of opulence and deprivation that motivated the rising mili-
tancy in strikes and marches among the campesinos, at great
personal risk. Many said: "I'd rather die struggling than die
of hunger."[7]

The National Guard was performing its traditional role
in the diocese, new bishop or not, ensuring that the campesinos remained amenable to the current state of affairs. Their
work was growing more complicated because of the pastoral efforts being undertaken by the diocese's priests and
catechists. Even Bible study came to be viewed as a subversive act in this period of rising frustration and expectation
among the poor. El Salvador's peasants were forming illicit
agrarian organizations to agitate for their rights and the
church was helping them do it.

Campesinos from all over the country came to San Miguel during the coffee harvest season. Romero was appalled by the spectacle of the poor littering the streets of the city, the landowners who would come to his Sunday Masses having made no provision for them. He began opening diocesan facilities to these economic refugees as a slightly better option than subsistence on the streets.[8]

Peasants and townspeople protesting election fraud or demanding justice for farmworkers were shot and killed in massacres across the country in 1974 at San Francisco Chinamequita, La Cayetana, Santa Bárbara, and other places as the state aggressively countered any opposition; others were rounded up by security, never to be seen again. A grim Archbishop Chávez dryly noted, in El Salvador "coffee consumes men."[9]

Violence that was breaking out in nearby dioceses in response to the organizing efforts of the farmworkers finally made its way to Santiago de María. In June 1975 six men and boys were brutally beaten, then murdered in Tres Calles, a village in Romero's diocese. The government said the peasants were members of an underground subversive organization who had been killed in a firefight after ambushing the National Guard, though no guard members were injured in the purported ambush. The villagers reported, however, that the victims, all members of one extended family, had been pulled from their beds, tortured, then murdered in cold blood with bullets and machetes. Their homes had been ransacked in a fruitless search for weapons.

Romero arrived on the scene just after the men had been buried, accompanied by a priest from the diocese, Pedro Ferradas.[10] Their blood still stained the walls of their homes, the floorboards "still held the stench of blood." It was a level of depravity and cruelty that he had never seen before firsthand. "In the years to come," Ferradas remembered, "we would become accustomed to such cruelties, but back then we were new to it."

Worse was yet to come. After attempting, mostly in vain, to comfort the grieving campesinos, alarmed at the anger he saw flashing in their eyes, Romero and Ferradas left Tres Calles and one scene of barbarity. It was not long before they stumbled upon another. A boy missing from the village had been found down the unpaved road away from Tres Calles, pulled from a ditch where the soldiers had left him. He, too, had been tortured, then executed. Romero left behind a community seething with anger, feeling bereft himself because of his ineffectual response. Passing in furtive silence a squad of National Guardsmen heading back toward the village where angry campesinos stood with machetes in hand, Romero felt a short flutter of the fear experienced on a regular basis by the villagers he had just left behind.

Walking back to his car, Romero was somber and silent. Reaching the presumptive safety of its interior, the bishop finally spoke. "Father Pedro," he said, "we have to find a way to evangelize the rich, so that they can change, so that they convert."[11]

The conversation is an early indication of Romero's understanding that the ones who need converting in El Salvador's bifurcated society would not be drawn from within the suffering community he had just attempted to comfort, but among the wealthy of El Salvador, whose addiction to privilege he was beginning to perceive as the source of the unspeakable misery he had just fled in Tres Calles. The raw acknowledgement on the road back to Santiago de María represents a first tentative step away from a model of pastoral intercession he had followed all his life, administering allocations of charity to balm the worst suffering of the poor he encountered, charity gleaned through appeals to the wealthy that were intended to produce a virtuous double-effect, to bring them closer to their own salvation. What is telling about the Tres Calles moment for Romero is the beginning of his understanding that what was wanted from the wealthy to give to the poor was not mere material charity, but a conversion of the heart that would allow them to understand that what the poor of El Salvador needed most was not a crumb from their table, but a seat at it; not charity, but justice.

Though he said nothing about his intentions to the campesinos at Tres Calles, Romero later visited the local Guardia commander to protest the massacre. The officer shrugged the killings off as a trivial accounting with local malefactors and, pointing a finger at Romero, he advised the bishop: "Cassocks are not bulletproof," perhaps the first time he would have his life threatened because of advocacy on behalf of the powerless. Within a few years, he would acquire a mountain of such threats.

Romero at that time was still unwilling to publicly criticize the government and make the church a source of political scandal, unable to believe that those authorities charged with promoting and preserving the common good could be aware that such brutality was taking place in the Salvadoran countryside. Romero wrote privately to President Molina, a deferential missive protesting the killings at Tres Calles and the indifference of the local Guardia officer.

In Santiago Romero would also begin a more serious personal effort to understand the socioeconomic underpinnings of the national crisis in El Salvador. At first anxious over the implications of Medellín, learning from the experiences of the poor instructed Romero in the relevance of the document and of its truthful evaluation of the signs of his times. Romero opened unused church buildings to serve as shelters to day laborers during the autumn harvest; he ordered that simple hot meals be offered them at night, discovering they were unlikely to be earning enough to eat properly despite all their backbreaking work for the region's wealthy.

In 1976 in one of several abortive attempts to avoid increasing social tensions, President Molina proposed a long-hoped-for land reform program, insisting that however forceful the opposition to the plan from the nation's landholding elite, the national government would not take "a single step backwards." Romero, taking the president at his word, urged the clergy and religious of his diocese to spend three days studying the agrarian reform proposals to discern how the church could support this opening. He organized seminars on the reform and sat in on the talks, accepting the schooling of his own subordinates and scrupulously scribbling in his notebook as the lecture progressed, his inner earnest seminarian once again coming to the fore. Rubén Zamora (who would go on to a prominent role in El Salvador's democratic resistance) was an expert on agrarian reform and the man Romero tapped to instruct Santiago de María's priests. "I'll never forget that image: me explaining the agrarian reform to all those priests, with Romero sitting at a student's desk in the front row, taking notes and listening to me super-attentively," he said. "The man wanted to learn."[12]

Since Bishop Romero had access to the powerful in El Salvador, he took the priests' criticisms of the proposed agrarian reform that emerged from their group study directly to President Molina, a personal acquaintance. Romero's enthusiasm for reform was betrayed within three months. Molina proved thoroughly unfaithful to his word: he not only took a step back, he sprinted away from his commitments to agrarian reform and the land redistribution it entailed after landholders openly and violently rejected the plan. Tragically this attempt at land reform would prove one of the nation's last chances at avoiding a deeper conflict, and

Romero, perhaps perceiving the peaceful alternatives to conflict dwindling before him, was profoundly disappointed.

His short experience in Santiago de María was fruitful, although the context was tragic, because Romero was reawakened to the dreadful reality of El Salvador's powerless and became acquainted with the "liberation" clerics he had previously suspected and feared. He began to see their "political" work as a natural, spiritually sound, and even required outgrowth of their pastoral work. More important, he came to perceive this work as thoroughly supported by recent church teaching emerging from Vatican II and Medellín. In Santiago Romero first denounced violence against people who had taken to the streets "in orderly fashion to petition for justice and liberty," just as he had denounced "the mysticism of violence" being preached by the revolutionaries. But perhaps the most poignant and profound impact of his short tenure in Santiago was Romero's discovery of the insight and wisdom, particularly in scriptural interpretation, of the poor and powerless. On several occasions, listening to the Bible commentary of "simple" campesinos, Romero came away impressed by what he heard and found that he learned something new himself about Scripture through the filter of their lives. For a man so innately trusting of authoritative sources, hearing the wisdom of the poor was a lightning bolt, one that partly motivated a new direction in his life and a certainty in his course that would help him prevail in the months of difficult accusations and challenges to his authority, even sanity, that lay ahead.

CHAPTER FIVE

Shepherd of His People

As Archbishop Luis Chavéz prepared for his retirement after thirty-eight years leading the Archdiocese of San Salvador, it was clear he had in mind that his primary deputy, auxiliary bishop Arturo Rivera, succeed him to lead San Salvador through what would plainly be a time of acute social turmoil. The retiring archbishop wanted someone in charge who understood the signs of El Salvador's complex and dangerous times.

The nation's campesinos had been the regular target of state-administered oppression on behalf of the landed elite for generations. But now for the first time, the church, because of its role in building up the human capacity and expectations of the poor, what Pope Paul VI had called the "authentic development of people," had likewise begun to feel the lash of repression. Nuns, priests, and parish catechists were receiving death threats; their homes were being searched and ransacked by the National Guard without warrant or explanation; several had already been picked up and tortured. Foreign priests had been arrested, abused, and tossed out of the country. The archdiocesan printing press, the St. Paul bookstore, and the Central American University had been bombed.[1]

Rivera was the preferred candidate among the priests working in the *campos* and with the increasing numbers of urban poor in San Salvador. By the end of his episcopal reign Chavéz had been seen as increasingly aligned with the "Medellín" priests who were confronting El Salvador's social injustice through efforts to organize the poor and develop leadership among the nation's campesinos. Rivera was widely understood to be the only episcopal candidate who would continue on that progressive path.

El Salvador's tiny class of landholders had become increasingly alarmed by the church's role in fostering "illegal" peasant unions that were agitating for better working conditions and wages and land reform. Chavéz was aware of efforts behind his back by the papal nuncio and leaders among El Salvador's military and agrarian elite—even among the other bishops in the Salvadoran conference—to petition Rome for an alternative candidate more to their liking. That man was Romero. Still, when it came, the decision from Rome stung. "It's curious," he told a diocesan confidante, "that the [Holy See] paid no attention to me regarding Monsignor Rivera, who was always my candidate and they knew it. Forty years as archbishop and they didn't take my opinion into account."[2]

While the upper class smugly rejoiced in the selection of Romero and the humiliation of Rivera, a groan of despair spread among the priests of the diocese who presumed that Romero would do his utmost to curtail their work among the people. It is true that the Romero who became archbishop was far from the man who would soon become beloved throughout the Americas as the "voice of the voiceless." One of his last acts as bishop of Santiago de María in fact was to issue a confidential memorandum in Rome detailing his concerns about the "politicization" of the clergy of El Salvador. The critical report, while acknowledging El Salvador as a nation that endured a "repressive military government" and "a cruel social differentiation in which a few have everything and the majority live in destitution," worried over the use of Marxist analysis by the priests in their dialogues and instruction with the campesinos and "political ideology" masquerading as scripture study among the justice-minded clerics.[3]

But what those supporting Romero as a "reliable" alternative to the "radical" Rivera did not know, because he had largely refrained from publicly expressing it, was Romero's growing alarm at the treatment of the campesinos he had witnessed in Santiago. His awakening to the suffering of the campesinos was not limited to concern over the physical and psychological harm they suffered at the hands of the National Guard. His natural pastoral interest in the welfare of the people was accompanied by a gnawing suspicion that the government itself was not a trustworthy ally in efforts to track down and prosecute the bad actors among the military and security forces in the countryside. He was coming to understand that the men of authority he had come to regard as friends were at least tacitly if not actively complicit in acts of suppression directed at the nation's subsistence communities and landless agricultural workers.

After years of clerical distance from the poor created by his own sense of episcopal decorum and enforced by the various hierarchal roles he had been asked to play, Romero had become reacquainted with the daily grind of El Salvador's landless laborers and the commonplace oppression of the nation's poor. In his two years in Santiago, Romero had crisscrossed the diocese on horseback. He revisited the poverty and desperation of his childhood and saw firsthand the suffering of the people, how the poor were not only driven into the hardest work for the lowest wages but were often actually paid far below the official minimum wage or cheated out of their wages altogether, then savagely beaten when they complained of such treatment. At a time when few imagined that Romero himself could be considered an adherent of a theology of liberation, he wrote in his diary: "The world of the poor teaches us that liberation will arrive only when the poor are not simply on the receiving end of handouts from government or from churches but when they themselves are the masters and protagonists of their own struggle for liberation."[4]

Oscar Romero was elevated to archbishop on February 22, 1977, a time of quickening crisis and conflict for El Salvador. Two days before he became archbishop of San Salvador, national elections pitted General Carlos Humberto Romero against a reform candidate, UNO's Colonel Ernesto Claramount Rozeville. The nation's campesinos and those who still hoped that justice could be achieved at the ballot box had come out in force to support Claramount, but the elections were marred again by blatant voter fraud and intimidation by government-sponsored paramilitary forces. General Romero (who was not related to the new archbishop) was declared the winner by a two-to-one margin.

Given the rushed selection process and the growing chaos in the streets of San Salvador, Romero's consecration as archbishop was a hurried, almost clandestine affair, especially compared to the majesty of his episcopal ordination just a few years before. It was conducted in a chapel in the San José de la Montaña Seminary, attended by the papal nuncio Gerada, a few bishops and regional diplomats, and a handful of priests and nuns who were mostly there to wish

Archbishop Chavéz a fond farewell. Perhaps the largest contingent of well-wishers were members of the Salvadoran elite among the military and from within the landholding and business classes.[5] Tellingly, with the streets of San Salvador boiling with fury over an election many judged fraudulent, no one from the government had been invited to attend the modest ceremony.[6]

In the weeks around Romero's appointment, priests had been arrested, others deported or refused entry into El Salvador. A Salvadoran-born priest was abducted, beaten nearly to death, then thrown through the diocesan chancery doors; and in the countryside brutality against the peasants who had tried to take advantage of outgoing President Molina's ill-conceived and swiftly abandoned land reform campaign continued apace.[7] San Salvador's Plaza Libertad filled with members of the opposition parties; many hundreds from Christian base communities from San Salvador parishes protested yet another stolen presidency as strikes and other demonstrations brought the capital city to a standstill.

Romero had been out of the city settling affairs in Santiago de María. He listened attentively to a last-minute appeal from Rubén Zamora that he return to San Salvador, that women and children were in the plaza, that violence was imminent, that perhaps if he were there with the people in the plaza the military would not have the nerve to violently clear the protestors out.

"I shall entrust you to God in my prayers," Romero told Zamora from Santiago.[8]

The government responded to the election fraud protests with violence, and scores were killed as the military broke up the remnants of the sit-in at the Plaza Libertad with bullets. It was left to the retired Archbishop Chavéz and his auxiliary Bishop Rivera to negotiate, along with the Red

Cross, a truce that allowed those seeking sanctuary from the military in a church near the plaza to finally escape on the morning of February 28. It would be just about the last time Romero would not be on hand when he was needed in San Salvador.[9] Protests and military counterstrikes and shooting continued throughout the day. The government acknowledged eight deaths, but as many as one hundred Salvadorans were killed that day according to tallies by the opposition.

This was the environment into which the cautious cleric Oscar Romero had been thrust, accepting a new role as shepherd of the entire nation. In his three short years as archbishop, Romero and El Salvador would endure a similar pace of almost ceaseless social tension and escalating violence until the murder of the archbishop himself opened the floodgates to more than a decade of civil war and suffering for the people of El Salvador. It would become Romero's fervent hope to avoid such an outcome; he knew the suffering of the poor in El Salvador's *cantóns*, its agricultural villages, would be staggering if they lost their only defender, the church. He quickly dedicated himself completely to preventing open war. In the beginning he believed that he could achieve this end as a mediator between El Salvador's wealthy—and their social enforcers within the military—and the mostly abandoned poor. The moment was quickly approaching, however, when he would be forced to take a more activist role; he would have to choose sides.

One of the last times Romero and his friend Rutilio Grande met was surely a frustrating moment for both. As the election crisis escalated on the streets of San Salvador, Romero had called a meeting of all his priests, his first as archbishop, to talk about the growing threat of Protestant evangelical incursions in El Salvador and had asked Rutilio Grande to lead the discussion. A state of siege had been declared and military water trucks were still hosing away the blood after the killings at Plaza Libertad as the exasperated and perplexed priests of the diocese convened.

As Grande attempted to lead the discussion on the baleful influence of Protestantism, priests were called away from the meeting to their parishes to attend to crises of missing persons. Reports of new violence kept interrupting the meeting. It wasn't long before Grande called off the discussion altogether to switch the topic to "other, more important things" happening just outside on the streets of the capital. Priests in attendance at the meeting said Romero seemed bewildered by the crisis quite literally engulfing him and the streets around him. The priests debated the best way to proceed, deciding to set up a network to exchange information about breaking events among themselves. "The doors of the archdiocese will be open all day and all night for any emergency," Romero finally offered as the meeting dissolved.

A little over a week later, he met with the priests and nuns of the diocese to discuss the status of the missionary priests, most of whom were not citizens of El Salvador and as a result were acutely vulnerable. Romero encouraged priests in hiding to return from the hills to their parishes, confident that the government intended to put an end to the chaos in the countryside. He urged the Jesuits of Aguilares, Grande among them, to continue their pastoral work, assuring them, "Since you are all Jesuits, I don't think anything will happen to you."

He took a departing Rutilio Grande aside to suggest they meet soon to discuss the whole experience in Aguilares where base community and campesino demands rose up together. In Aguilares the campesinos were rising up, not only demanding better wages but, perhaps more threatening to the sugarcane plantation owners who relied on cheap labor, were seeking their own land through agrarian reform and attempting to organize themselves into agricultural collectives. Those alternative structures might mean liberating themselves from the backbreaking poverty of landless harvesters. To the landholders they were an existential threat inspired by communists masquerading as priests. Romero was worried over the radicalism of some organizations and suggestions from clerics of the possibility of violence.

Before he had left his previous episcopal post, senior priests in Santiago had solemnly warned Romero that Aguilares had become a cauldron of communist agitation and impressed upon him his episcopal obligation to clear the agitators out. Confronting his old friend Rutilio about his role in pastoring Aguilares into the state it was had already been a heavy worry to him.

Grande agreed to make an appointment with his new archbishop soon to discuss conditions in his community, "God willing." That meeting was never to be.[10]

Perhaps the first thing to understand about Rutilio Grande and Oscar Romero is that the two men were friends, and that was something that did not come easily to either of them. They met when Romero came to San Salvador as secretary to the bishops' conference in 1967, ten years before Grande's assassination. Romero lived for a time at the diocesan seminary where Grande served as prefect. They shared a shyness around others, and among the emerging, Jesuit-trained vanguard of priests who would soon become the leaders of the base community revolution in the Salvadoran countryside, Romero felt acutely out of place. His discomfort among the younger priests and seminarians was obvious and noticed, some compared him to a "shadow" in the manner he lurked about the seminary, "clinging to the walls," and he interacted little with the seminarians or with their Jesuit teachers.[11] He seemed in fact to go out of his way not to interact with them. One Jesuit remembers, "He would go down to the dining room at different times so that he wouldn't run into us. It was clear he was avoiding us and that he'd arrived at the seminary laden with prejudices."[12]

But with Rutilio he was able to make a connection, and for his part Grande was able to recognize a sincerity and spiritual depth in Romero that made it easy for him to overlook their differences on pastoral policy and Salvadoran politics. Beyond their natural reserve, the two men shared a grounding in Jesuit spirituality; sadly they also shared psychological problems and anxieties that had been a burden to them throughout their adult lives. They both experienced periods of depression and moodiness that forced them to withdraw from other people and to assume too much of the burden of the duties of their various appointments—in fact often the duties of other less scrupulous clerics who worked with them. Romero's stubborn need for perfection and correctness bordered on the compulsive. (His mental state was at different times used in whispering campaigns meant to discredit him.)

Periodically Romero suffered from exhaustion that was propelled by his perfectionism and workaholism. Even as a young parish priest in San Miguel, he was always trying to take on more than he should rightly bear. A parishioner recalls how Romero used to work all hours, leading rosaries and hearing confessions through the day and late into the night. One night a woman asked the driven priest what penance she should do.

"You should pray five pesos," the exhausted Romero mumbled.

"He had fallen asleep!" the parishioner recalled. "That's the way he was. He would work without stopping until he was totally burned out."[13]

Grande's psychological problems were perhaps more se-
vere. After the end of his seminary studies he had been sent
by the Jesuits to complete his theological education in Spain
where he had suffered two serious breakdowns. Despite
doubts about his potential to succeed in the demanding
world of the Society of Jesus, Grande was able to hold himself together despite milder bouts of melancholia, depression, and irritability throughout his life. In fact, he was
successful as a Jesuit. In his role as teacher and prefect of
students at San Salvador's diocesan seminary and as one of
the leaders of the Jesuits' pastoral rejuvenation, he helped
shape two generations of priests.[14]

The two men surely had shared a complicated friendship.
Despite his connections to the Jesuits, Romero had campaigned against the order on several notable occasions, and
he had been among the Salvadoran bishops deploring the
"political" contamination they charged the Jesuits represented. After Grande had delivered a fiery sermon denouncing
the social order in El Salvador during the annual patronal
Feast of the Divine Savior Mass at the Metropolitan Cathedral in 1970—a final mark of his irredeemable radicalism to
many—Romero had been among the nation's prelates who
blocked Grande's appointment as rector of the national seminary. (Asked in 1976 to deliver the same prestigious sermon,
Romero had become personally alarmed by the obvious social
injustice he witnessed as bishop of Santiago but took the
opportunity to denounce the influence of "rationalistic, revolutionary, hate-filled christologies," presumably courtesy of
the Jesuits.)[15]

But when Romero was selected to become a bishop in
1970, he gratefully accepted Grande, soon to be the exem-
plar of the emerging model of church leadership and whatever this new idea of liberation theology might mean for

El Salvador, as the master of ceremonies for his ordination celebration. That decision was a signal—perhaps even an unconscious one by Oscar Romero—that this new bishop, despite his inherent conservatism and natural caution, was unhesitant about reaching out in unexpected ways when it meant a natural expression of his affection and respect. But his friendship with Grande did not mean that he wasn't worried about the nature of the Jesuit's ministry at Aguilares and the way it was perceived by the elite of El Salvador.

Rutilio Grande was a bridge for Romero to the younger, activist priests of the archdiocese whom he was struggling to understand and to a new, emerging, and radical interpretation of Christ and liberation that Romero was struggling to grasp. When this bridge was demolished, presumably Romero should have fallen into the abyss; instead he was carried over to the other side where Grande had been beckoning him.

Grande was Romero's voice crying in the wilderness, preparing the way not only theologically through his advanced study of the emerging trends in the church, but also pastorally. Grande was deeply impressed by the concept of Christian base communities. He became the innovator of this pastoral approach in El Salvador and a mentor for a generation of young pastors. His was a ministry that Romero did not completely understand until its violent, shocking end. It became the ministry Romero accepted for himself, even as he almost immediately recognized its heavy obligation.

But perhaps to Romero's surprise, this new responsibility itself seemed a liberation that became quickly evident in the transformation it effected in San Salvador's pastor. Indeed, many of the people assembled for Mass on the night Grande was killed believed they heard Rutilio himself speaking through Romero. Romero's liberation, one that allowed him to finally fully embrace the wisdom of Medellín, became the liberation he was in turn able to offer to the people of El Salvador, to oppressed and oppressor, a liberation not effected through political and social change alone, but through conversion and penance, what he came to propose as a liberation of transfiguration.

The weeks leading up to Grande's assassination were certainly a period of increasing tension and danger for priests simply attempting to perform their pastoral duties in El Salvador. Several foreign-born priests had already been brutalized and expelled; the Jesuits were regularly threatened and interfered with; the menacing slogan, "Be a patriot, kill a priest," had already been put into circulation in flyers and alleyway graffiti. But how many priests in El Salvador up to Rutilio Grande's murder truly accepted that their work among the poor was putting their lives at risk? Probably many suspected that the worst they could anticipate was a beating, a public humiliation, or deportation. It is no small thing to kill a priest in a nation as infused with Catholicism as El Salvador, but resentment against the church and against the agents of change at the local level that many parish priests had become had been building within certain circles of Salvadoran society for years. Besides, deeper than the church in the Salvadoran psyche lingered the phantasm of the *matanza* and the dark, murderous panic and fear of the peasantry it excited. Some were ready to act.

Grande had been a thorn in the side of local planters for years. He had brought the concept of Christian base communities into Aguilares in 1972. The experience was electrifying for these indigenous and mestizo campesinos. To describe them as poor would have been extravagant. If they had land at all, it was the rockiest or the highest or an eroding plot alongside the sheer face of a mountainside. Grande and his fellow priests brought empowerment to these people through gestures as simple as asking for their opinion of the state of their own lives; they brought them Bibles, taught them to read, and asked them if they really believed that it was the divine will of their loving Father in heaven that they should wallow on earth within this utter destitution and hopelessness. Was this how God wanted his children to live?

When these campesinos embraced the obvious, that no, it was not God's will that they should suffer so, that they had inherent dignity as people of God, they began to understand that it was up to them to do something about it, to come to God's assistance in building his reign of peace and justice on earth. They formed agrarian committees and demonstrated for land reform and better treatment from the patrons of the harvest.

This was the threat, this was the "violence" that aroused the ferocious wrath of the landholding elite through their instrument the National Guard; this was the "communism" that the Jesuits and foreign Third World priests were disseminating among the good campesinos of El Salvador. It was Bible reading and Scripture study; literacy programs, improved nutrition and health programs; the guidance of loving pastors as they reached a deeper understanding of their own faith, their precious lives, their God-given human dignity, and the idea of justice in this life—not as a material reward for *lucha* and persistence—but to help God cocreate a community of justice and mercy.

Naturally Grande had to die for such offenses.

With the faint and then thwarted hope of land reform in the region coming and going, Grande had accelerated his criticism of the local elite and deplored the economic and political vulnerability of the community's subsistence farmers. He had been warned; he persisted in spite of the warnings.

Just a few weeks before his murder, Rutilio had commented wryly during a homily on the recent expulsion of

Colombian priest Mario Bernal. "I am fully aware that very soon the Bible and the gospels will not be allowed to cross the border," he said. "All that will reach us will be the covers, since all the pages are subversive . . .

"I'm afraid that if Jesus of Nazareth came back, coming down from Galilee to Judea, that is from Chalatenango to San Salvador, I daresay he would not get as far as Apopa [where Father Bernal had been abducted], with his preaching and actions. They would stop him in Guazapa and jail him there. . . . They would accuse him of being a rabble-rouser, a foreign Jew, one confusing people with strange and exotic ideas, against democracy, that is, against the minority. Ideas against God, because they are a clan of Cains. They would undoubtedly crucify him again."

As the death threats mounted, "We have to hope that the cassock protects us," Grande told a *New York Times* reporter. "They have never killed a priest."[16]

But as the disappearances of others who had raised their voices in appeals for change continued, and the bodies piled up on the dead-end alleys of San Salvadoran barrios and garbage dumps without investigation or prosecution, some were growing more confident that there was little risk in acting—now, not even against a priest. These cycles of violence had repeated regularly throughout the history of El Salvador; its campesinos had for generations lived in a state of constant, subdued terror. Now that the priests had thrown their lot in with the poor, the conspirators of the night seemed to have concluded, why should priests remain exempt from the fate of the poor?

Grande had been born in El Paisnal, the town he was traveling to on March 12, just three weeks after Romero's installation as archbishop. He was going to his birthplace to join the community for the second day of the novena of San José. He would not make it to the village alive.

Three bloodstained children ran to Marcelino Pérez. A Jesuit and assistant to Grande at El Paisnal, Pérez had given up his seat in Grande's jeep to allow "old Manuel" and Nelson, a fifteen-year-old epileptic boy who sometimes rang the church bells, to ride with Grande. On the way, they had stopped to offer a lift to the children who sat in the back. "They killed Father Tilio," the children told him. "The father's done for; he's not talking anymore."

Pérez soon discovered it was true. Grande had been struck by a hail of bullets at close range; Manuel appeared to have been trying to cover the priest's body with his own, his protecting arm was tattered by bullets. Poor Nelson had been executed with a single shot to the forehead. The three screaming children had been allowed by the assassins to flee the car unharmed.

Romero had spent the afternoon of Grande's murder in his characteristically, up to then, hesitance mode, reviewing with Bishop Rivera a statement that was intended to be read at all the Masses throughout the diocese on March 13. The Salvadoran bishops, in a show of unity that would not be repeated while Romero lived, had denounced the government's assault on those protesting the election in Plaza Libertad. But now that the statement was on the verge of being heard in his churches, Romero was beginning to worry that it might appear too one-sided, that the statement went too far, that it might sow confusion, that it might do more harm than good.[17]

He did not know that the time of church timidity, acquiescence, and silence had already passed. The phone rang; it was outgoing President Molina on the line to tell the archbishop personally of the slaying of the priest on the road to El Paisnal, to insist that the government had nothing to do with the murders, to assure the archbishop that a thorough investigation of the murders would be forthcoming.

What had been the meaning of the death of Rutilio Grande to Oscar Romero? For many, who had believed Romero a boring, even tiresome, predictably conservative appointment to shepherd the church in El Salvador through these precarious times, the killing of this Jesuit priest was the signal of an abrupt rupture, for the old Romero was cast off completely and a new Romero emerged: empathetic, soulful, and courageous. Jesuit Father Jon Sobrino remembers this conversion of Romero's was described by some in the Salvadoran church as "Rutilio's miracle."[18] If so, what a sacrifice Rutilio Grande was asked to make in order to move his bishop to a life with, of, and for the poor of El Salvador.

Sobrino suggests that, in meditation over the lifeless body of his friend and supporter and the two innocents unlucky enough to have accompanied Grande when the assassins found their target, the scales fell from Romero's eyes and the methods and message that Rutilio Grande personified, so troubling before to this cautious prelate, became clearly identifiable with the ministry of Christ in the world. Just as Jesus had given up his life for others, Rutilio had offered up his own. Was Romero prepared to do the same?

That night as he thought about the people of Aguilares, the broken bodies of Grande, an old man, and a peasant boy crucified with high-powered rifles, Romero perhaps understood in a visceral way the new teaching he had been struggling with from the Vatican council and Medellín: what it meant to have a preferential option for the poor and to join with the people of God in their sorrow and suffering, as Rutilio had done, up to the ultimate expression of identity and surrender, offering up his earthly life. "The will of God," Sobrino remembered, "must have looked very different to Archbishop Romero that night in the presence of those three bodies and with hundreds of campesinos staring at him wondering what he was going to do about what had happened."[19]

The killing of a priest had been shocking enough; the killing of this, a rare friend, must have been a terrible blow, yet Romero comported himself calmly and with dignity throughout the ordeal, attending immediately to the community at Aguilares, concelebrating a spontaneous funeral Mass among the Jesuits and campesinos who gathered around Grande's body and that of an old man and teenage boy. That night Romero began a practice that would become a consistent feature of his episcopacy. He turned to the priests and laypeople in mourning gathered around him and bluntly asked for help, for guidance. He was entering uncharted waters both as a man and as a bishop. "What should the church do? How should the church respond?" Jon Sobrino remembers being shocked to be asked for direction by an archbishop, particularly this one, but also "feeling great tenderness for that humble bishop, who was asking us, practically begging us, to help him bear the burden that heaven had imposed on him . . ."[20]

Before driving back to San Salvador, after conferring with the Jesuit provincial and other priests in El Paisnal, Romero determined to offer a common funeral Mass at the Metropolitan Cathedral for the three dead. Two days later in San Salvador, at Rutilio's Mass, Romero lamented the loss of his friend, a friend who had been by his side during the "peak moments" of his life. How odd it must have seemed not to have him on hand to confer with during this moment of crisis for the Salvadoran church. He told the one hundred or so concelebrants, the crowd spilling out of the church and into the square beyond its doors, and the thousands huddled over radios in bodegas and homes all across the city and countryside of El Salvador that, "all of us who remain on pilgrimage," must gather what message they could from the death of Rutilio Grande.[21]

The day after Grande's funeral the clergy of the archdiocese and the national bishops' conference met separately to determine how best to respond to Rutilio's murder. The idea of the single Mass for the entire archdiocese the following week surfaced and immediately became the object of intense debate. Romero's attentive, patient listening during eight hours of debate over this bold gesture represented another dramatic break from the authoritarian tendencies of his past—and a shock to those expecting a taciturn, decisive prelate. But like his "conversion," the apparently abrupt change in style actually reflected a process, with connections to his spiritual practices and psychoanalytic explorations that had begun much earlier. In Santiago de María, he had opened diocesan buildings to provide shelter to the community's homeless harvest workers and had many times walked among them as they prepared their nightly rest, hearing their troubles and consoling their despair but mostly learning how to listen.

In Santiago, during these improvised lessons in the political economy of El Salvador, Romero had begun to question decisions he had made in the past and had begun to really listen, not only to his priests, but also the people of his parishes, hearing wisdom from them that he came to deeply respect. Now after hours of sometimes contentious debate, Romero accepted the idea of a single Mass for the entire diocese at the Metropolitan Cathedral. It would be a show of unity that would also serve as a marker to the political establishment that the church, clearly now among the targets of the status quo, was associating itself directly with the persecuted of El Salvador. It was a striking gesture; and it would be immediately challenged from within and without the church. Business leaders demanded that Romero drop the idea. The papal nuncio Gerada was especially unhappy with the idea, which he deemed "provocative and dangerous" and perhaps a violation of canon law. He made repeated attempts to persuade Romero against the gesture; Romero refused to back down on the decision.

The following Sunday, during the "single Mass," the cathedral and the plaza before it were bursting with people, more than one hundred thousand, who had come to Mass, many for the first time in years in the largest assembly of Salvadorans ever up to that time.[22] All of the priests of the archdiocese concelebrated with the papal nuncio Gerada, and Romero's homily was enough to dispel any of the doubt and worry that may have lingered among those of his priests who remained suspicious that Romero had been sent to be an obstacle to their work among the poor. Romero had heard plenty of the stories of "communist priests" with a handgun in one hand and a Bible in the other rousing the countryside against the landowners since becoming archbishop. Hadn't he told many of them himself just a few short months ago?

At the altar of the Metropolitan Cathedral, mourning over the body of his friend, he addressed those rumors directly. "Let no one impede the church from telling humankind that there is reason to hope in the church," he said during his stirring homily. "Let no one abuse our language and attempt to justify with the gospel other doctrines that are not Christ's doctrine. . . . in front of the archdiocese gathered here, in light of the unity that has brought us together at this one Mass, I want to publicly thank all of these beloved priests. Many of them risk their lives, and like Father Grande offer the greatest sacrifice."

Here Romero was interrupted by applause. He seized on it. "That applause ratifies the profound joy that I feel in my heart as I take possession of this archdiocese," he said. "I also feel that my own weaknesses and my own inabilities find their complement, their power, and their courage in these united priests. Beloved priests, remain united in the authentic truth of the gospel. This is another way to say to you, as Christ's humble successor and representative here in the archdiocese: the one who attacks one of my priests, attacks me."

The message Romero newly embraced was contained in Pope Paul's *Evangelii Nuntiandi,* an apostolic exhortation offering to all those who struggled for human dignity in the so-called developing world the accompaniment and support of the church. That was a message that Grande had long ago already taken up into his heart. The church's message to lift up and defend human dignity, Romero told his rapt audience, is a message of faith, without which "all will be feeble, revolutionary, passing, violent." But with faith, he assured the people, the liberation that Grande preached, the liberation he embodied was true liberation "and because it is often misunderstood, even to the point of homicide, Father Rutilio Grande died," joining hundreds of campesinos whose disappearances had passed with little notice except to people like Grande and now Romero.

As the single Mass ended, with thousands of people applauding him, "You could see him grow stronger," Inocencio Alas, a diocesan priest, remembered. "It was then that he crossed the threshold. He went through the door. Because, you know, there is baptism by water, and there is baptism by blood. But there is also baptism by the people."[23]

Romero had left behind forever the women serving tea and talking charity; he had turned down the offer of a mansion fit for an archbishop in San Salvador; he had refused the gift of a fancy car and driver. He had returned to be with the humble people of his childhood.

It is a poignant irony that Rutilio Grande's death, orchestrated by men who believed they could somehow put a stop to the social dynamic that Grande and priests like him had set in motion, had instead awakened the spirit of a priest who would become their greatest "enemy" and a most eloquent voice of the voiceless.

Rutilio was the first priest to die as the conflict in El Salvador heated up; he would not be the last.

CHAPTER SIX

A Nation in Crisis

As archbishop, Romero became engaged in a mortal struggle to preserve unity within the church, restore Salvadoran society, and make real the commitments of the church as a force of spiritual and material liberation for the oppressed people of Latin America. His ministry would be fraught with personal danger and subject to physical and rhetorical attacks. His priests would be brutalized and killed, his people victims of escalating violence or driven by the same into the embrace of revolutionary factions. Romero came to understand El Salvador as the piteous embodiment of the oppressive historical forces identified by the Latin American bishops at Medellín. He also came to see its "true vocation" to be a "land of salvation," an example of a way forward in solidarity and peace out of that morass, one that he suspected he would not—and did not—live to see.

The single Mass in San Salvador was the first of a series of bold gestures that would firmly set the tone for Oscar Romero's short, dramatic tenure as archbishop. These acts would not be cost-free; the single Mass in particular marked Romero as a provocateur to many within the hierarchy and

Salvadoran society at large, permanently troubling important relationships for the new archbishop. Romero was forced to explain his decision to a scolding papal nuncio in what would be a first appearance on the carpet before a frowning, uncomprehending curial bureaucracy.

Following through on another commitment that emerged during that dramatic week's marathon consultation with his priests, Romero also ordered that all the Catholic schools in the archdiocese be closed for three days of study and reflection on the crisis conditions of Salvadoran society and the killing of Grande. This naturally generated an uproar among the well-to-do parents, who now not only had restless children on their hands but worries about "communist" indoctrination direct from the archdiocese itself.

Romero also issued a statement that as a representative of El Salvador's persecuted church, he would refrain from attending, and thereby institutionally blessing, any government ceremony or official event until the repression of the countryside ceased and murder of Rutilio Grande was properly investigated. It never was, and Romero remained true to his word. This was an especially pointed gesture as it meant he would not attend the upcoming inauguration of the new president, despite pressure from some scandalized fellow Salvadoran prelates about the statement that absence would make. Romero, ever scrupulous, even declined invitations to other events at which he might be photographed socializing with El Salvador's political or military leaders. That meant the next year turning down an invite from the already antagonized papal nuncio Gerada for a celebration of the new papacy of John Paul I.[1] Needless to say, Romero's scrupulosity was not appreciated by the nuncio, who was far less concerned about being photographed with El Salvador's elite even as the church's casualties rose higher.

Romero's homily at the single Mass electrified his radio audience. It was the beginning of what would become a powerful media ministry for the new archbishop and would become a hallmark of Romero's pastoral outreach.

As the eight o'clock morning Mass began in the Metropolitan Cathedral, streets emptied and radios clicked on, not only throughout San Salvador, but throughout the nation, from campesinos gathered around a battery-powered transistor to the wealthy gathered around a living room hi-fi. The Monseñor's broadcast included loyal listeners among the military—even among cells of revolutionaries in the cities or peasant battalions in the Salvadoran jungle. Everyone tuned in to hear what the Monseñor might say during the Sunday homily.

But it was not only for spiritual sustenance that Romero's homily became one of the most closely listened to radio programs in El Salvador. Romero read the *hechos de la semana*, "the events of the week," to his countrymen each Sunday as part of his homily, which became a spoken Sunday newspaper. With the government or the wealthiest families controlling virtually all other mass media in the nation, from newspapers to televisions to radio networks, the archdiocese's YSAX had become the only trustworthy source for real news and specifically for some account of the increasing ranks of the disappeared. According to listener surveys at the time, seventy-three percent of the rural population and forty-seven percent of the urban regularly tuned in to the Mass from the cathedral to hear the homily. The station itself became a regular target of the Salvadoran military, which jammed its signal; twice the station was demolished by bombs. After the second time YSAX had been blown up, and typical of the familiarity and affection Romero instilled in the people of San Salvador, a cab driver, spotting Romero sitting in a car pulled up next to him at a stoplight, took two dollars from his pocket and thrust it upon the archbishop: "Para la radio, Monseñor," he said.[2] The archdiocesan newspaper *Orientación* likewise became a rare outlet for actual news about the repression strangling the nation and for alternative opinions. It became so identified with resistance, however, carrying *Orientación* itself became a dangerous act of defiance that could lead to a beating or worse from the National Guard.

He had barely made it through two months as archbishop when whispering campaigns against him were already reaching curial corridors in Rome. The papal nuncio made no effort to disguise his disdain for the decisions the new archbishop was making; relations with his one-time friends and supporters among the upper class had quickly soured and the government's suspicions of Romero were only equaled by his own doubts about the intentions and complicity of government officials in the mounting oppression.

Romero hoped to head off the critical narrative reaching Rome and meet with Pope Paul himself to explain his decision-making. In Rome, he helped prepare an exhaustive report on the events in El Salvador and the church's response. While waiting for what proved a grilling from Vatican officials still smarting over Romero's refusal to back down to the papal nuncio Gerada over the famous single Mass, Romero sought some calm before the upcoming storm with a walk along the Via Della Conciliazione, the dome of the Vatican lit up in the evening distance. Father César Jerez had been sent to Rome to assist the archbishop. Like other priests of the archdiocese he had been wondering how to account for the change in the man who had become their unexpected savior. He screwed up the courage to put the question to Romero during their walk.

"We all have our roots," Romero told Jerez, El Salvador's Jesuit provincial. "I was born into a poor family. I've suffered hunger. I know what it's like to work from the time you're a little kid." That life was interrupted by years of studying first in the national seminaries, then as a young man in Rome. He recalls becoming "absorbed in my books."

"I started to forget about where I came from. I started creating another world," he explained. When he finished his studies and returned to El Salvador his life as pastor of paper continued when "they made me the bishop's secretary in San Miguel. I was a parish priest for twenty-three years there, but I was still buried under paperwork."

"And when they sent me to San Salvador to be auxiliary bishop, I fell into the hands of Opus Dei, and there I remained." Then he was finally given a real pastoral appointment: "They sent me to Santiago de Maria," he said, "and I ran into extreme poverty again. Those children that were dying just because of the water they were drinking, those *campesinos* killing themselves in the harvests. . . . You know Father, when a piece of charcoal has already been lit once, you don't have to blow on it much to get it to flame up again. And everything that happened to us when I got to the archdiocese, what happened to Father Grande and all. . . . it was a lot. You know how much I admired him. When I saw Rutilio dead, I thought, 'If they killed him for what he was doing, it's my job to go down that same road.' . . . So, yes, I changed. But I also came back home again."[3]

After being battered by Cardinal Sebastiano Baggio, secretary of Congregation of Bishops, he endured more admonishments from the secretary of state office, where a curial operative suggested Romero remember the "prudence" with which Jesus Christ conducted his public life.

"If he was so prudent, then why was he killed?" Romero wanted to know.[4]

He finally made his way through the curial gauntlet to meet privately with Pope Paul following the regular Wednesday general audience. Romero presented the pope with a photograph of Rutilio Grande and attempted to put into words his efforts in the archdiocese and the tensions he was confronting.

Romero was greatly heartened by the message he received.

The pope seemed to sense the conflicting swirl of powerful forces engulfing the inexperienced prelate. "Courage!" Pope Paul told Romero, grasping both of his hands. "You are the one who is in charge!"[5]

He would be in need of that courage. He would be coming home to a church divided within itself and to a nation confronting an accelerating cycle of violence and recrimination that as archbishop he would strive heroically to interrupt.

During his trip to Rome, Romero continued to work on his first pastoral letter as archbishop (he would participate in three more). "The Paschal Church" was his attempt to make sense out of the horror and trial confronting the church in El Salvador. Romero seems to have written this deeply personal epistle himself.[6] "Christ's church has to be an Easter church," he wrote, "a church that is born of Easter and exists to be a sign and instrument of Easter in the world. . . . The church does not exist for herself. Her raison d'être is the same as that of Jesus: service to God to save the world."

He noted that the sense of this Easter church is contained in the papers released after the 1968 Medellín conference. "[The bishops at Medellín] kept well in mind the fact that the Spirit of Easter urges the church to dialogue with, and to serve, our peoples. 'We are,' they said, 'on the threshold of a new epoch in the history of our continent. It appears to be a time full of zeal for full emancipation, of liberation from every form of servitude, of personal maturity, and of collective integration.' The church cannot be indifferent, they proclaimed, when faced with 'a muted cry [that] pours from the throats of millions of men, asking their pastors for a liberation that reaches them from nowhere else.' "

Romero said that the archdiocese was living its "paschal hour." It would endure, even flourish, as long as it remained able to tap into "the spiritual riches of Easter, that greatest inheritance of the church."

"I see that there is already being achieved among us here what was expressly desired by the bishops at Medellín, when they were speaking to young persons: 'That the church in Latin America should be manifested, in an increasingly clear manner, as truly poor, missionary and paschal, separate from all temporal power and courageously committed to the liberation of each and every person.' "

He wrote, "Beloved brothers, sisters, friends. We have together lived through a Lent that was a Way of the Cross and a Good Friday that has come to full flower in this bright and hopeful hour of the Easter of resurrection. Those of us—bishops, priests, religious, and laity—who are aware of what it means to be a church, the depository of all the energies working for the salvation of humanity in Christ, also understand the challenges and the risks of these difficult times. The major challenge arises from the hope placed in the church by the world. Let us be worthy of this hour."[7]

Romero's "statements" as archbishop, however, were not limited to the rhetorical. In his daily life he demonstrated his sense of how to be a church of and for the poor. As archbishop, Romero made a point of physically breaking down barriers. He frequently went out to visit with the people in their communities, installing a loudspeaker on his ramshackle Jeep to better reach them. He dropped everything to meet with his parishioners, typically the most humble campesinos who sometimes walked for days to reach San Salvador and tell the Monseñor their sorrows and troubles. He had a snack bar built in the archdiocesan offices. It became a homey refuge and meeting place for staff and priests stopping by for conferences and finally for anyone visiting the chancery. Romero himself began joining his priests and visitors there.

The modesty of his own living arrangements was another small statement of his personal liberation from the expectations and temptations of his position. Having declined the offer of a bishop's residence, Monseñor Romero decided to live on the grounds of the Divine Providence Hospital among people suffering from cancer, who were cared for by Carmelite sisters. Over the years he had visited and dined with the sisters when he visited San Salvador and had taken a liking to the hospital site.

He made a small room for himself in the sacristy behind the chapel. The papal nuncio stormed in one afternoon to lecture Romero about his latest outrage only to be scandalized further by the archbishop's humble "residence."[8] Even that small gesture had political ramifications. Donations to the hospital from San Salvador's wealthy fell off, much to Archbishop Romero's regret, and the sisters themselves became targets of street harassment by virtue of their association with the "subversive" archbishop.

For Romero personally, escalating harassment was not limited to shouts of "Red!" or "Communist!" from upper-class thugs on the street. He was frequently harassed at army checkpoints as he attempted to complete his everyday pastoral work, visiting the parishes and communities of the archdiocese. The soldiers no longer showed any respect for the position of archbishop and seemed to seek out ways to humiliate him. Thuggery also came in the form of print ads and newspaper columns that accused the archbishop of collusion with communist revolutionaries, even of acts of terrorism himself.

Worse than the attacks from outside the church walls was the isolation within. Romero had generated esteem, even affection among the priests of the archdiocese who had low to negative expectations of him when he became archbishop. But among his brother bishops, several of whom had surreptitiously lobbied Rome for his appointment, he had become the object of scorn and criticism. The church had become divided not only between its pastoral workers and priests in the fields and El Salvador's episcopal hierarchy, but within the hierarchy itself. A divide had opened between bishops, Romero and Rivera—who saw no choice but for the church to align itself with the people, the poor and the increasingly outspoken popular organizations that represented them—and the rest of the conference, adhering to old episcopal scripts of faithfulness to order, stability, and authority purportedly represented by government and the social status quo. As a result, throughout his three years as archbishop, Romero was constantly at public and private loggerheads with essentially the entire bishops' conference of El Salvador in frequently breathtakingly petty and on occasion mortally perilous disputes.

A quartet of bishops from the Salvadoran conference sought to undermine Romero within El Salvador and in communiques to the Vatican behind his back. His meetings with the bishops' conference were brutal exercises in self-control. Romero's brother bishops attacked him and, for the most part, he silently endured their criticism. His only reliable ally during such encounters was Bishop Rivera, the man he had been rushed into service to replace. He was at times driven to despair, even tears, by the disunity among the bishops.

Outright insubordination—essentially illegally seizing control of Caritas food distribution from Romero's hands—led him to remove Vicar General Bishop Marco Revelo in November 1978, but Romero most often found himself butting heads with Bishop Pedro Arnoldo Aparicio of San Vicente. At the Puebla conference in Mexico in impromptu press conferences, the two men could have been describing two different nations. In Aparicio's El Salvador, Romero was a pawn of Marxists, Jesuits were scheming to provoke violence, rebel priests were training child revolutionaries, and "the disappeared" were leftists in crafty hiding or escaped to the countryside to join the guerrillas.[9] Aparicio was close to the economic and military elite of El Salvador, even closer than Romero had been, and became his fiercest critic, frequently alleging that Romero's preaching amounted to a subversive threat to the social order. His targets were not limited to Romero, however. The nation's other "subversives," according to Aparicio, included the members of the Society of Jesus and his own diocesan priests. In a memorable sermon in September 1979 after the murder of yet another priest, Father Alirio Napoleón Macias, Aparicio essentially denounced his own diocesan priests. His condemnations were eagerly reprinted in the morning papers.

Romero notes in his diary, "[Aparicio] says that he cannot defend them and almost accuses them himself, exposing them to possible assassination. He says that the priests who have been killed were purged by the left and that there are priests committed to the left who cannot pull back without the left killing them."[10]

Aparicio and the other bishops of the conference did not limit their attacks on Romero to their own pulpits and the local, Romero-loathing media, however. In frequent reports to Rome, they poisoned his relationship with many in the Curia. Their reports even reached Pope John Paul II. After his experience as a priest in communist Poland, the pope had developed a deep-seated suspicion of anything that smacked of socialism and he was too ready to listen to concerns about communist intrigues in the archdiocese.

While his struggles within the church hierarchy persisted, outside the chancery walls a campaign against forces that challenged social privilege continued to take a gruesome toll.

CHAPTER SEVEN

Love, the Vengeance of Christians

Confronting the increasing violence of Salvadoran society became a sorrowful, regular task for Archbishop Romero. "Oh, if we only had men of prayer among those who guide the destiny of the nation and the fate of the economy," he said during a homily in July 1977. "If, instead of relying on human devices, people would rely on God and on his devices, we would have a world like the one the church dreams of, a world without injustices, a world with respect for rights, a world with generous participation by all, a world without repression, a world without torture."[1]

Though the attacks of the death squads and the general repression helmed by the National Guard were the usual targets of his denunciations, El Salvador's revolutionary factions were just as capable of violence of their own—and were also chastised by Romero. In April 1977 one group, seeking the release of political prisoners held by the government, abducted Foreign Minister Mauricio Borgonovo, a member of one of the "catorce," the 14 families. The Molina government steadfastly refused to negotiate with the kidnappers. The Borgonovo family asked Romero to intervene, and the archbishop publicly appealed to the FPL (in English the "Popular Forces of Liberation") to release the foreign minister.

In a homily on May 8, 1977, Romero began what would become the great tightrope act he would be called to make as archbishop of San Salvador. "We are in solidarity with the anguish and the hope of the people of our time, especially those who are poor and suffer [and] we are not being political when we speak in this way. The council has stated . . . . : 'The church has the right to pass moral judgments, even on matters touching the political order, whenever basic personal rights or the salvation of souls make such judgments necessary.' When I was a student in Rome, I was moved by the following words of Pope Pius XI: 'The church is not involved in politics, but when politics touches the altar, the church defends the altar.'

"One side accuses the church of being Marxist and subversive," Romero said. "Another group of people wants to reduce the church to a spirituality that is separated from the realities of the world, a type of preaching that remains in the clouds, that sings the psalms and prays, without any concern for earthly affairs.

"This is what we preach," Romero told the assembly: "No to vengeance! No to the class struggle! No to violence! Only a blind person would believe that in times of violence and persecution the church has been lacking in solidarity with those who suffer, whether that person be rich or poor. We have defended the life of the chancellor, Borgonovo Pohl, and we were happy to do so. We did not want him to become a victim of violence. Therefore, together with the mother of Borgonovo who is suffering, the church is in solidarity with all those mothers whose children have been taken prisoner, with all those who suffer."

On May 11 Borgonovo's body was found dumped on a roadside outside of San Salvador. Romero said the homily during Borgonovo's funeral Mass, and when he assured the grieving family and friends that the church rejected violence and that its ministers did not preach violence, he was greeted with furious derision. The assembly came close to outright catcalls and boos. To the upper class, Romero had become little better than a revolutionary in a cassock, no matter his outreach to them, his calls to conversion. Up and down the street in front of the church, the flyers littered the street: "Be a patriot. Kill a priest."[2]

That afternoon a death squad from the White Warriors Union took up the suggestion. Just a few months after Rutilio's murder, Father Alfonso Navarro Oviedo was gunned down in his rectory compound. He had been well-known to the people of El Salvador and to its military for having said a Mass in the Plaza Libertad hours before the ruthless termination of the demonstration there after General Romero's "election." As a young man of thirty-five, Father Alfonso had been pastor of the Church of the Resurrection, serving a San Salvador neighborhood of middle-class people. His opinions were well-known and his catechetical instruction had been controversial; Navarro had been threatened on a number of occasions. In February the garage of the parish house and Navarro's car had been destroyed.

According to the official report lodged by the Organization of America State's Inter-American Commission on Human Rights: "On the afternoon of the murder, [Navarro] had been at the presidential residence, summoned because of information against him in connection with classes that he was giving at a high school in the capital city. He then went to the archbishop to report and then went home. A few minutes after he arrived, some four men called at the residence. A young boy [Luis Torres] opened the door and they shot him. Father Navarro ran out to the yard in an attempt to climb over the wall. He was cut down by seven bullets. Even so, he was still alive when found, but died at an Aid Station at 3:30."[3] According to those who sought to save his life, Father Navarro managed to offer forgiveness to his murderers before he died.

Once again Romero was forced to offer the homily at a funeral Mass for one of his priests. "There is a story about a caravan that was traveling through the desert and being guided by a Bedouin," he began, speaking to those gathered in Navarro's Resurrection Parish and listening on the radio all over the country. "They had become desperate and thirsty and were searching for water in the mirages of the desert. Their guide said: 'Not there, over there.' He had spoken these words so many times that the members of the caravan became frustrated, took out a gun, and shot the guide. As the guide was dying, he extended his hand and said one last time: 'Not there, over there.' He died pointing the way.

"This legend becomes a reality in our midst: a priest . . . dies forgiving and praying for his assassins . . . Father Navarro shares with us his message. Let us receive this message." Romero continued, "We, as priests, live with a hope. We cannot be communists because they have mutilated this hope in a life hereafter. We believe in God; we preach a hope in this same God, and we die convinced of this hope. This then, is the second part of Father Alfonso Navarro's message: Hope is an ideal that never dies. It is like the guide in the desert who extends his hand and says: 'Not there, not for those mirages of hatred, not for that philosophy of an eye for an eye and a tooth for a tooth—no, that is criminal. Over there: "Love one another." '

"Do not walk on those roads of sin and violence," Romero said, finishing his sermon, "you are going to build a new world, so walk on the road of love."

His first bloody month of May as archbishop was not over. A little more than a week after Borgonovo's execution, the National Guard, in an effort smugly code-named "Operation Rutilio," was called in to the late Father Grande's community of Aguilares to chase off members of a peasant-rights group that had seized unused land. The campesino organization fled the scene as two thousand noisy troops approached. In their frustration at missing the preferred target, the soldiers turned on the community of Aguilares itself. After several campesinos fired on the approaching soldiers, killing two, the troops began a rampage, murdering perhaps fifty on the spot, raping the community's women and pillaging its humble homes.

The soldiers stormed the parish church where Grande's body had lain, blasting the tabernacle with rifle fire, kicking communion wafers into the street. The National Guard occupied the town. They took hundreds away for interrogation; they abused those who remained. Those with pictures of Grande or crucifixes in their homes were especially mistreated, and the soldiers turned the church into a barracks.[4] The three remaining Jesuits in Aguilares were arrested, shackled, and deported.

When Romero tried to visit the devastated town, he was barred entry by the National Guard. He complained about his treatment in a letter to the outgoing president Molina, noting first that he struggled to understand how a person who proclaimed himself a Catholic could "permit the outrageous abuses that are being committed by the nation's security forces." He wrote, "I do not understand, Mr. President, the reasons that military authorities could possibly have for not allowing me to go in person to the Aguilares church to see for myself what was happening. . . . Can it be that even the person of the archbishop is seen as a danger to national security?"[5]

The town remained militarized for weeks. When Romero was finally allowed to enter Aguilares, he celebrated Mass before a traumatized community. As archbishop, he said, "gathering up the bodies of those who have been abused, the victims of this persecution of the church" had become a regrettable part of his duties.

"Today I have come to gather up this church and convent that has been profaned, this tabernacle that has been destroyed and above all else to gather up this people that has been humiliated and unnecessarily sacrificed. . . . I bring you the word that Jesus commands me to share with you: a word of solidarity, a word of encouragement, a word of orientation and finally, a word of conversion."

After the Mass, Romero, carrying the Blessed Sacrament, led a procession to resanctify the community following its desecration. The procession was stopped at one point by a wall of National Guard troops, rifles pointing into the crowd. At the rear of the procession, Romero became aware of the soldiers ahead. "*Adelante*," he told the people. "Go ahead." The soldiers gradually fell away before the people advancing together. The moment embodied the hope and the courage that Romero fed his beleaguered people and the trust they had quickly learned to place in him. It was also a small indication to dangerous men how much the timid archbishop had changed in just a few short months. This new authority did not go unnoticed.

Father Navarro's slaying had been vicious, but it paled against the violence visited upon another priest murdered by security forces the following year. The loss of Father Octavio Ortiz was especially painful to Romero. He had known Ortiz since he was a teenager in the seminary, a young man much like himself, of modest background, determined to rise above his presumptive station and become a priest. Ortiz was the first priest Romero ordained as a bishop.

He records in his diary: "A very tragic day. It dawned with the news that there had been a military operation in El Despertar in the parish of San Antonio Abad. It was at a house frequently used for retreats designed to deepen the participants' Christian faith. Father Octavio Ortiz . . . was leading a program of introduction to the Christian life for some forty young men.

"But at dawn today, the National Guard with a riot squad set off a bomb to break down the door and then entered violently with armored cars and shooting. Father Octavio, when he realized what was happening, got up just to meet his death, as did four other young men. . . . Father Octavio's face was very disfigured; it looked like it had been run over and flattened by something very heavy." The government tried to claim that the teenagers and young men on retreat had opened fire on the National Guard from the roof of the building; they even arranged their bodies there for a photo opportunity with San Salvador's compliant press. It was all a story concocted to cover up the military's ruthlessness and denounced as such on the airwaves by the archbishop. At the morgue, Romero wept over the body of Father Ortiz, cradling his crushed head and praying over the corpse, assuring with the words of 2 Timothy 4:7: "Octavio, my son," you have completed your mission, you have kept the faith.[6]

If this was the treatment the National Guard felt secure in doling out to priests in El Salvador during these months, one can imagine the horrendous suffering of the countryside where, far from the eyes of international media, the campesinos of El Salvador endured much worse. It was a concern never far from Romero's mind. In campaigns to root out armed revolutionary groups the military would sweep through villages; whole families would be liquidated, and entire communities would fade away into the mountains.

Hosting a Bible study, speaking with a foreign journalist, or joining a farmworkers' organization were just some of the offenses that could cost a man and his family their lives. If the members of ORDEN, the Organización Democrática Nacionalista (National Democratic Organization), a paramilitary organization of army reserve units and campesinos recruited or forced to act as snitches and capos against the people of their own communities, did not conduct their own brutal enforcement operations, they were connected to people who could. No one knew when an unguarded comment would invite a nocturnal visit from plainclothes members of the National Guard. Some men took to sleeping out in the wild, away from their families and homes, hoping in this manner not to be "disappeared" during the night.

A visiting American journalist got a small glimpse of what the daily terror in the countryside was like. "On my first trip to Cabañas, Father [Cesar] Jerez had provided me with a guide—a young Christian activist—and with him I listened and asked questions in whispers as the villagers snuck into a mud-wattle house where we were hiding. The Orden snitches, who were members of their own communities, were all around us, they warned, and they were risking their lives by talking to us. One by one, the victims told the stories of how the killers had taken away one woman's son and slit his throat and of how another woman had found her husband in a ditch, 'chopped into little bits' by the machetes of the killers, so that she could not even bury his body whole. Finally, they produced statements—this was the Jesuit influence at its most distinctive—meticulously written out in pencil, in which they detailed the date and time of each attack, and listed the treasures that 'los Orden' had pillaged from them. 'I was robbed,' a typical statement would say, 'of a dozen oranges and four candles. And they cut up the ropes of my cot, so that I have no bed.' "[7]

Death squads focused on the still illegal campesino organizations that had flowered in the aftermath of Scripture study and instruction by parish priests and catechists, presumed by the military to be a lifeline to the revolutionaries. In the cities, bodies showing signs of terrible torture, mutilation beyond the recognition of family and friends, were dumped in allies and garbage heaps, men and women deemed subversive or related to subversives by the unknown puppet masters of the death squads. Many of these victims were connected to political resistance groups but many others were merely community organizers, even church catechists.

The suffering and persecution of the church, too, would continue. The right-wing clandestine White Warriors Union issued an ultimatum to El Salvador's forty-seven Jesuits, ordering them out of the country within thirty days and assuring after that point it planned to hunt down and kill any who remained. After consulting with the Jesuit community in El Salvador, Secretary General Pedro Arrupe, SJ, replied, "They may end up as martyrs, but my priests are not going to leave because they are with the people." In one of the few instances where the government intervened to protect El Salvador's priests, President Romero ordered soldiers posted outside Jesuit schools and residences. The Jesuits came to no harm—this time—when the deadline passed, inadvertently revealing, however, how powerful people within the government were connected to death squads like the White Warriors.

After collecting a few death threats personally from the White Warriors Union, Father Rafael Palacios twice came to Romero to express his concerns about his safety in Santa Tecla, where he worked with grassroots Christian communities, and where the death squad master-builder Roberto D'Aubuisson schemed on his family farm. Romero indulged the worried priest but, perhaps indicative of how common such threats had become, thought Palacios's fears were somewhat exaggerated. On June 20 Palacios was gunned down on the street in Santa Tecla in retaliation for the murder of a National Guard officer.[8]

"We can present, along with the blood of teachers and laborers and campesinos, the blood of our priests," Romero said during Palacios's funeral Mass. "This is communion in love. How sad it would be, if in a country where such horrible murders are being committed, we were not to find priests among the victims. They are the testimony of a church incarnated in the problems of her people."

Romero was one of the first bishops called upon to breathe life into the documents of Vatican II, Medellín, and Puebla. What had been theological theory and spiritual rhetoric, locating the church with the oppressed, the poor and vulnerable, Romero had to make real. When he did, even those who had formulated the teaching documents that were underpinning the church's contemporary outreach to the modern world were uneasy over the results. But to Romero, a radical witness beside the poor was the only logical, inevitable outcome of the contemporary teaching. How many bishops have so memorably—so vulnerably—stood before such remorseless forces of material, psychological, and physical oppression? How many have been such a willing and joyful defender of the poor? He quickly went beyond the church's teaching documents, however, learning from real life in real time that the true prophet, the true manifestation of the church in modern times, the body of Christ in the world, was located among the most vulnerable and the most oppressed.

"The world does not say: blessed are the poor," Romero said during a homily on January 29, 1978. "The world says: blessed are the rich. You are worth as much as you have.

But Christ says: wrong. Blessed are the poor, for theirs is the kingdom of heaven, because they do not put their trust in what is so transitory."

At Belgium's University of Louvain, where he received an honorary degree, Romero spoke to his growing admirers in Europe. In a speech that became an apologia for his life and his vision of the church, Romero said, "The world of the poor, with its social and political characteristics, teaches us where the church must incarnate herself in order to avoid that false universalization which always ends up in a connivance with the powerful. The world of the poor teaches us how Christian love should be. . . . The world of the poor teaches us that the magnanimity of Christian love must respond to the demand of justice for the majorities and not flee from the honest struggle. The world of the poor teaches us that liberation will occur not only when the poor become recipients of government or church benefits but when they themselves become authors and protagonists of their struggle and their liberation, thus unmasking the ultimate root of false paternalisms—even ecclesial ones."

At Louvain, Romero issued what amounts to a synopsis of Salvador's suffering, a cry for help to Europe and the West, a summary of the case against the oppressors in El Salvador, a news bulletin to those in the first world or within the hierarchy who had been so determinedly blind to what had been transpiring in El Salvador and a defiant, impassioned defense of his mission to be a church with the poor, of the poor. It reads like a well-structured final argument of a defense attorney, yet it is Romero speaking, and the man on trial is himself.

"While it is clear that our church has been the victim of persecution during the last three years, it is even more important to observe the reason for the persecution. It is not that just any priest or just any institution has been persecuted. It is that segment of the church that is on the side of the poor and has come out in their defense that has been persecuted and attacked. The persecution comes about because of the church's defense of the poor, for assuming the destiny of the poor.

"Where the poor begin to live, where the poor begin to liberate themselves," Romero said, "where men and women are able to sit down around a common table and share, there is the God of life. . . . This faith in the God of life is what explains the depth of the Christian mystery. To give life to the poor, one must give from his own life, indeed give even his own life. The greatest sign of faith in a God of life is the witness of a person willing to surrender his own life. 'There is no greater love than this: to lay down one's life for one's friends' (John 15:13)."

Romero was coming to view the poor as the chief instructors of contemporary faith, both in the testimony of the conditions of society reflected by their daily struggle and the scriptural wisdom they personally shared. And through that wisdom he was coming to understand the necessity of the church to engage with its times and not absent itself on history's sidelines muttering spiritual pieties. Of course, he would say, the church has no choice but to stand up for those who are being oppressed and demand redress from their oppressors. The church is in conflict with the government, he said in December 1978, because "we take the people's side." And that meant sharing the risks endured by the defenseless.

"A church that doesn't provoke any crises, a gospel that doesn't unsettle, a word of God that doesn't get under anyone's skin, a word of God that doesn't touch the real sin of the society in which it is being proclaimed—what gospel is that?" he asked.[9]

In his second pastoral letter, Romero wrote, "[The] church is the Body of Christ in history. . . . Christ founded the church so that he himself could go on being present in the history of humanity precisely through the group of Christians who make up his church. The church is the flesh in which Christ makes present down the ages his own life and his personal mission.

"That is how changes in the church are to be understood. . . . The church can be church only so long as she goes on being the Body of Christ. Her mission will be authentic only so long as it is the mission of Jesus in the new situations, the new circumstances, of history. The criterion that will guide the church will be neither the approval of [the powerful or the threatening]. It is the church's duty in history to lend her voice to Christ so that he may speak, her feet so that he may walk today's world, her hands to build the kingdom, and to enable all its members *to make up all that has still to be undergone by Christ*" (Colossians 1:24).

"I am glad, brothers and sisters," Archbishop Romero said at Father Palacios's funeral Mass, "that our church is persecuted precisely for its preferential option for the poor and for trying to become incarnate in the interest of the poor and for saying to all the people, to rulers, to the rich and powerful: unless you become poor, unless you have a concern for the poverty of our people as though they were your own family, you will not be able to save society."

But Romero understood his pastoral mission was not limited only to seeing the victims and "gathering up the bodies." His job was far more complicated. He challenged himself repeatedly to convert people who had come to idolize what he called "the mysticism of violence" on both sides of the struggle. "Let there be no resentment in your heart," he told the people of the now twice-brutalized Aguilares.

"May this Eucharist, which is a call to be reconciled with God and with our sisters and brothers, satisfy our hearts with the knowledge that we are Christians. May it remove from our hearts every trace of hatred and rancor."

Even as the skies over the countryside and cities of El Salvador grew red with the blood of new victims of violence meant to suppress the rising expectations of the landless and left behind, he never ceased hoping for a conversion among the powerful that he was convinced could bring about justice and peace in El Salvador. In January 1980, two months before his assassination, he said, "To the oligarchy, I repeat what I said before: do not look on me as a judge or an enemy. I'm only the shepherd, the brother, the friend of this people, the one who knows of their suffering, of their hunger, of their affliction.

"In the name of their voices, I raise my own to say: do not make idols of your riches; do not preserve them in a way that lets others die of hunger. One must share in order to be happy."

His misgivings about liberation theology and his prior difficulties in accepting the practical and spiritual implications of Medellín had been well-known. As archbishop, Romero quickly found himself increasingly perceived as the embodiment of "progressive" elements within the Central American clergy even as he protested that he was merely locating the church where it ought to be, where it needed to be, in service to the poor and the defenseless. That perception drew equal parts acclaim and scorn. An entire weekly newspaper was devoted just to piling fabrications and attacks on the archbishop, whom it dubbed: "Oscar Marxnulfo Romero."

At the Mass in Aguilares, he said, "Let us be firm in defending our rights, but let us do so with love in our hearts. For if we act with love, then we show that we are seeking the conversion of sinners. Love is the vengeance of Christians." These brief words capture the essence of Romero's "political" struggle for peace, a growing confidence that the church would only be true to the Gospel and to its new theological commitments through maintaining a strong, honest voice amid the nation's deepening conflict. This would not be a voice of a radical temporal or social liberation, but a voice of spiritual and merciful liberation for all.

The attorney for the archdiocese and director of its legal aid office, Roberto Cuéllar, in a recent documentary remembers Monseñor Romero as "not one of those great thinkers or defenders of liberation theology. Romero was a theologian of the beatitudes," Cuéllar says. "Give food to the hungry; give drink to the thirsty. Visit the persecuted in prison; give strength to the weak. What impressed me about him was his ability to make the beatitudes real—to defend the rights of the poor and later their human rights as well."

In November 1977 Romero defended his pastoral ministry to the many and powerful enemies who had rhetorically and to a great extent physically encircled his office since he become the voice of El Salvador's voiceless: "We have never preached violence, except the violence of love that left Christ nailed to a cross. We have never preached violence except the violence that we must each do to ourselves to overcome selfishness and such cruel inequalities among us. The violence we preach is not the violence of the sword, the violence of hatred. It is the violence of love, of brotherhood, the violence that chooses to beat weapons into sickles for work."

Yes, he told his fellow priests and the rest of the people of God, the church hears the cry of the poor and the church understands the social structures of sin in El Salvador; it appreciates the material need that is crushing the poor, the politically outcast, and powerless. But it also understands that as much as these social deficits need to be addressed, the salvation of El Salvador's "sinners" in the military and landholding class, brothers and sisters to the suffering, and the restoration of Salvadoran community likewise remained a pastoral responsibility of the archdiocese.

"Let us pray for the conversion of those who have beaten us and those who had the audacity to sacrilegiously profane the tabernacle," Romero said in Aguilares. "Let us pray for the conversion and repentance of those who have made this place a prison and a torture chamber. May the Lord touch their hearts before they hear the Lord's sentence: all who take the sword will perish by the sword. May they truly repent and behold the ones they have violated. May a wellspring of mercy and goodness be poured forth upon all of us and enable us to realize that we are all sisters and brothers."

It is at this juncture, frequently noted by the archbishop, where his vision of liberation and that of some adherents of the emerging liberation theology perhaps go their separate ways. Romero was not interested in promoting a clash of classes and social status, of violently reordering El Salvador's maldistribution of wealth or hereditary property crimes. He was concerned with saving bodies and souls among his brothers within the poorest and most vulnerable communities, but also among the upper classes untouched by the violence of poverty and willfully blind to their complicity with it. His denunciations and imploring addresses were aimed not at dividing and castigating, but restoring the faith—and the community of faithful—offering hope to the oppressed and entreating and welcoming wayward Christians back into the community of the people of God.

Romero explained, "When they tell me that I am a subversive and that I meddle in political matters, I say it's not true.

I try to define the church's mission, which is a prolongation of Christ's. The church must save the people and be with them in their search for justice. Also, it must not let them follow ways of hatred, vengeance, or unjust violence. In this sense, we accompany the people, a people that suffers greatly. Of course, those that trample the people must be in conflict with the church."[10]

But like the loving father, waiting, praying for the return of his prodigal, Romero remained attentive to those among his flock who participated or benefited from the oppression of the poor, in prayerful hope that one day their eyes and hearts might be opened, a reconciliation achieved, and the community restored. "Let us not tire of preaching love," Romero said during his homily on September 25, 1977. "Though we see the waves of violence succeed in drowning the fire of Christian love, love must win out; it is the only thing that can." This is the hope embodied by the archbishop that today in El Salvador still awaits its fulfillment. Part of Romero's legacy is that in joining with the God of history, the God of justice and mercy, confidence in that hope can continue across lifetimes if need be, if one may only die in faith as he did.

CHAPTER EIGHT

The *Locura*

Romero was frequently called to grisly scenes in San Salvador, sometimes to discover to his horror the body of an old friend—or the disfigured remains of a new one from among the campesino leaders whose wisdom he had come to greatly appreciate. So many corpses were found abandoned in alleys and streets, in neighborhood garbage dumps, Romero caustically pronounced, "It seems that my vocation is to go around picking up bodies."

This was not an entirely figurative statement. By some estimates, between 1979 and 1981 death squads were responsible for the killing of more than thirty thousand people. Comforting the survivors of government torture and family members of victims and the disappeared almost became a daily part of his pastoral work in the archdiocese. Spying an exhausted peasant woman waiting for him without complaining in a hallway of the chancery—many walked for days to meet and be comforted by the Monseñor—Romero would drop everything to speak with this mother of the murdered or missing—often to the consternation of those charged with the thankless task of keeping him on schedule.[1]

Confronted with the macabre spectacle of violence being visited on the poor, impressed by the example of Nicaragua where a popular uprising, against all expectations, had overthrown the brutal Somoza regime, Romero had tentatively come to accept that the oppressed people of El Salvador had the legitimate right to defend themselves against the merciless violence orchestrated by the military, a principle that would muddy the nature of his martyrdom years later. He based that acceptance on both the catechism's acknowledgment of a right of self-defense and contemporary Catholic teaching.

In *Populorum Progressio* Pope Paul VI had left open a tiny "except where" legitimacy to the "right" of insurrection against tyrannical authority. "Everyone knows," Pope Paul VI wrote, "that revolutionary uprisings—except where there is manifest, longstanding tyranny which would do great damage to fundamental personal rights and dangerous harm to the common good of the country—engender new injustices, introduce new inequities and bring new disasters. The evil situation that exists, and it surely is evil, may not be dealt with in such a way that an even worse situation results" (31).[2]

But accepting an opening to defensive force did not mean the archbishop encouraged or welcomed it. Romero knew that in an all-out civil war the defenseless Salvadoran people would be caught in the middle between the revolutionaries and the military, and it was the people who would suffer the most for it. It was a position he tried to explain in a fourth pastoral letter, "The Church's Mission amid the National Crisis," which explored the church's relationship with the popular organizations, primarily campesinos rights groups, then erupting across the country. The groups ran the gamut of popular resistance to El Salvador's existing political and economic order. Some groups, particularly those more aligned with the church, were purely peaceful;

others, grown frustrated after repeated cycles of local and national election fraud and years of brutal oppression, had openly turned to violent resistance. In "The Church's Mission," he denounced the idols of wealth and national security, but just as vehemently the idol of popular organizations that remained fixed on a material liberation effected by a violent overthrow of the status quo.

The recent bishops' meeting in Puebla, Mexico, had adjourned with a statement urging the church to "recognize the suffering features of Christ the Lord" in the face of "children, struck down by poverty," the indigenous or Afro-American, the peasants. That commitment, Romero wrote in "The Church's Mission," was borne out in the statistics tracked by his Legal Aid office. The letter reported that in just six months "the number of those murdered by various sections of the security forces, the armed forces, and the paramilitary organizations rose to 406. The number of those arrested for political reasons was 307." Romero writes, "Not a single victim comes from the landowning class, whereas those from among the campesino population abound. Faced with this oppression and repression, there arises naturally what Medellín called the 'explosive revolutions of despair,'" a despair that produces a spiral of violence "racing toward hitherto unsuspected levels of cruelty."

"It is making increasingly problematic the likelihood of resolving the structural crisis peacefully. It has reached the stage where it seems we are engaged in a real civil war. It may be informal and intermittent, but it is nonetheless pitiless and without quarter. It tears apart normal, everyday life, and brings terror into every Salvadoran home."

In the face of these perilous conditions, Romero writes, the church has to be true to her evangelizing mission, pursuing justice in peace but remaining a forceful prophet against "the rapid death of repression or the slow death (but no less real) of structural oppression."

"The church, then, would betray its own love for God and its fidelity to the gospel if it stopped being the voice of the voiceless, a defender of the rights of the poor, a promoter of every just aspiration for liberation, a guide, an empowerer, a humanizer of every legitimate struggle to achieve a more just society, a society that prepares the way for the true kingdom of God in history. This demands of the church a greater presence among the poor. It ought to be in solidarity with them, running the risks they run, enduring the persecution that is their fate, ready to give the greatest possible testimony to its love by defending and promoting those who were first in Jesus' love."

Picking up the famous commitment codified in Puebla, "this preference for the poor," Romero writes, "does not mean an unfair discrimination between the various classes of society. It is an invitation to all regardless of class, to accept and take up the cause of the poor as if they were accepting and taking up their own cause, the cause of Christ himself: 'I assure you, as often as you did it for one of my least brothers, you did it for me.'"

Per Puebla and Medellín before it, Romero continued to highlight not just the sins of individuals who committed violent acts, but the structural sin and violence embedded in the privileges of the Salvadoran elite. "It is sad to read that in El Salvador the two main causes of death are: first diarrhea, and second murder," he said. "Therefore, right after the result of malnourishment, diarrhea, we have the result of crime, murder. These are the two epidemics that are killing off our people."[3]

He condemned "the idolatry that exists in our country. Wealth is made a god, private property is absolutized by the capitalist system, national security is made the highest good by the political powers who institutionalize the insecurity of the individual."

He took the church's evangelizing message of peace and change into the streets of San Salvador. He even met clandestinely with leaders of guerrilla forces to try to persuade them of the power of Christian nonviolence in the face of oppression. On an afternoon in March 1979, he met with representatives of a guerrilla group and tried to persuade them to the Christian ideal of nonviolence.

"But these people are firmly convinced that it is not the force of love that will resolve the situation, but rather the force of violence," he recalled in his diary. "They do not want to listen to reason, much less hear about Christian love. I realized that there is a very deep gap between the way a whole sector of our society, represented by these people, thinks and the Christian position."

Romero wrote, "I ask God to light the way for his Church so that it be understood even by those who want the good of the country but use very different means than those Christ taught us."[4]

Meeting with guerrillas was just one of the many unorthodox responsibilities of the omnipresent archbishop. Romero's diary offers a jaw-dropping glimpse into the complex and dangerous world he inhabited. Assailed on all sides by need and discord, he seems somehow to draw energy and conviction from the chaos and crisis swirling around him. Just as in San Miguel when he set his mind to setting the diocese in order, Romero proved an indefatigable administrator and pastor in San Salvador. Remember that beyond the political gauntlet he was required to run each day, Romero still had a diocese to run and a straining host of committees and bureaucracies to confront and set right. He reformed the archdiocesan Caritas operation, reinvigorated its publishing and radio media, created new programs to respond to the special pastoral needs of his times, and yet remained attentive to the many mundane responsibilities of his office, the blessing of new sanctuaries, the daily *embrazos* with his parishioners, and the settling of clerical squabbles.

Romero somehow still maintained the vigor to respond to the ceaseless litany of crises that came to his door: negotiating with kidnappers, guerrilla leaders, union representatives, and business owners; resolving the various sit-ins and seizure at the Metropolitan Cathedral; raising money to feed campesinos hiding in the Salvadoran mountains; and even arranging to hide traumatized victims of political violence at the national seminary. One wonders if the so-called conversion of Romero's psyche had some supernatural effect on his physique as well. Where did he find the mental and physical stamina? Like any other natural son of San Miguel, Romero slung a much-used restorative hammock in a room in his domicile at Divine Providence, but the true secret to his mental and physical endurance, according to intimates, was his prayer life. Despite all the demands made upon him, Romero kept, perhaps steeled by his Jesuit spiritual discipline, to a regular, determined daily appointment with prayer and contemplation.

While Romero managed his archdiocese with growing confidence, the "other Romero," the general charged with managing the nation, was having less success with his national responsibilities. The short, illegitimate administration of General Romero had succeeded in a little more than two years in accelerating the social discord and level of barbarism deployed against campesinos and those unfortunate enough to be deemed disloyal to patria in El Salvador. President Romero had promised reforms and failed to deliver them.

He agreed to free political prisoners only to stand by indifferently as scores of them were "disappeared" in the night by military death squads as quickly as they were released.

In the general's first year in office, close to seven hundred political deaths were recorded; the next year almost two thousand were killed. Strikes and demonstrations created disorder in the streets; capital flight sucked the monetary lifeblood out of the economy. General Romero's own brother, a retired teacher, became a reprisal victim, gunned down, along with three members of his household, including an eight-year-old stepdaughter, by one of the armed popular groups. As the disorder threatened to throw the entire society into chaos, in October 1979 the general was removed in a bloodless coup by moderate members of the army's officer corps. In a last-ditch effort to stave off all-out civil war, the officers promised to make real reforms. The coup leaders formed a junta with civilian members of the political opposition who had been fraudulently denied victories in recent elections. The hope of the people for a peaceful resolution to the nation's conflict rose quickly as El Salvador's new leaders promised land reform that would mean redistributing some of the nation's wealth and power and the end of the hated ORDEN.

Romero let hope overcome good judgment, and lent his credibility, perhaps too freely, to this junta. Like the people, he was tired of the violence and saw the junta as a last chance at justice and peace. But the reform-minded officers were never able to assert control over the military, and the bloodletting continued.

The popular resistance groups, seeing little positive change from the junta, accelerated their programs of resistance and the spiral of recrimination and violence only turned faster. Civilians who had agreed to join the junta, fearing that they were being used as cover for a new round of oppression, began resigning in protest against the escalation of violence by security forces and paramilitary organizations. Romero held off as long as he could, believing he needed to give the junta a chance to succeed, before he too began to publicly denounce the "reformist" junta as much as he had the administration of his ousted presidential namesake.

In Washington, the Carter administration, still recovering from the shock of the Sandinista victory in Nicaragua, was alarmed at the growing disorder in El Salvador. It feared the likelihood that the unmitigated repression visited on the unions and farm laborers' organizations and the farcical dead end that Salvador's ruling class had made of democracy would inevitably lead to another successful "socialist" revolution, this time in El Salvador. The president's advisors believed the United States could help guide the junta to a softer landing that might preclude an all-out revolution and the beginning of a Central American version of the long-feared domino effect, as a socialist revolution in one state encouraged the same in others.

Now, concerned that the junta seemed on the verge of losing complete control of the countryside, it was considering something more significant: $5.7 million in military aid. Romero was horrified by the prospect of sophisticated US weapons flowing into the hands of people who had already proved themselves capable of so much brutality. In 1976, Candidate Jimmy Carter had made commitment to human rights a key rallying point during his campaign. Romero reasoned that after all the estimable rhetoric on human rights, surely now that he was president Carter would be sympathetic to his appeal.

"Because you are a Christian and because you have shown that you want to defend human rights," Romero wrote on

February 17, 1980, "I venture to set forth for you my pastoral point of view in regard to this news and to make a specific request of you.

"I am very concerned by the news that the government of the United States is planning to further El Salvador's arms race by sending military equipment and advisors to train three Salvadoran battalions in logistics, communications, and intelligence. If this information from the papers is correct, instead of favoring greater justice and peace in El Salvador, your government's contribution will undoubtedly sharpen the injustice and the repression inflicted on the organized people, whose struggle has often been for respect for their most basic human rights. . . . As a Salvadoran and archbishop of the Archdiocese of San Salvador, I have an obligation to see that faith and justice reign in my country. I ask you, if you truly want to defend human rights:

—to forbid that military aid be given to the Salvadoran government;

—to guarantee that your government will not intervene directly or indirectly, with military, economic, diplomatic, or other pressures, in determining the destiny of the Salvadoran people."

Romero, noting the country's "grave economic and political crisis," assured Carter that the people of El Salvador were "awakening and organizing and have begun to prepare themselves to manage and be responsible for the future of El Salvador, as the only ones capable of overcoming the crisis."

He added, "It would be unjust and deplorable for foreign powers to intervene and frustrate the Salvadoran people, to repress them and keep them from deciding autonomously the economic and political course that our nation should follow."

Romero read the letter during his Sunday homily on February 17, 1980, to great applause from those gathered in the cathedral. In his diary that night, he explained that it was not just the increasing level of violence that worried him so much, prompting the desperate attempt to intervene with the North American president, it was the "style" of the growing conflict. Romero recognized something happening in El Salvador that most of the world was willfully ignoring—certainly in Washington and in Rome: the evolution of an unnaturally brutal tone in the conflict, something ancient re-arising in El Salvador, something perhaps truly satanic.

This "new notion of special warfare," Romero wrote, "consists in eliminating in murderous fashion all the endeavors of the people's organizations under the pretext of fighting communism or terrorism. This type of warfare means to do away not only the men directly responsible, but with their whole families, which in this view are all poisoned by these terroristic ideas and must be eliminated." Romero wrote that his letter was "designed to beg" President Carter not to send any more military aid to El Salvador since that "would mean great harm to our people, because it would be destined to snuff out many lives."[5]

It wasn't just that Salvadoran security was liquidating political opponents and helpless campesinos presumed to support forces threatening to the state—certainly this was bad enough. Worse, though, was the manner, the brutality of many of the slayings that troubled Romero. Victims were tortured sometimes for weeks before they were killed, bodies were mutilated, helpless women savaged, and children murdered. It was not enough for soldiers to seize Father Octavio Ortiz and the young men unfortunate enough to have joined him for a retreat that awful weekend and murder them. No, Father Ortiz's face had been blasted off, his body riddled with bullets and run over by a tank. It was a theater of terror deliberately contrived to escalate a climate of fear among the lower rungs of Salvadoran society. It was a kind of macabre brutality that had been strategically deployed to suppress Salvadoran campesinos for decades.

In this time of Romero, however, the campesinos had been "liberated" by Scripture; they perceived the church, through Romero, at their side. They were emboldened by hope. Furthermore, in the 1970s they had been joined by an educated, emerging professional and business class that would not be so easily terrorized into submission. Perhaps because the usual formula of brutality was proving less effective, the elite who encouraged the bloodletting and their invisible "death squad" army felt obliged to ratchet up the violence to new levels of depravity, drawing for the first time the appalled attention of the international media.

In their historic review of the conflict, U.N. researchers were overwhelmed by the fury and the nature of the violence they uncovered. "In examining the staggering breadth of the violence that occurred in El Salvador, the Commission was moved by the senselessness of the killings, the brutality with which they were committed, the terror that they created in the people, in other words the madness, or *locura*, of the war."

Monseñor Romero had understood early in the conflict that coming "locura."

Unlike Jesus in Gethsemane, when Romero began to contemplate the likelihood of a violent death he did not want for watchers and protectors in the garden. Quite the opposite. So many warnings came his way from those worried over his personal safety, so many imploring that he not travel alone, walk the streets of the capital, even leave the confines of his residency in which some foolishly believed he could remain safe. No, Romero had too many friends and coworkers, even the Carmelite sisters at his residence, willing to watch and wait with him. So many that he began to fear for their well-being. At a meeting in early March 1980, US Ambassador Robert White informed Romero of death threats against him. An OAS report notes that although the archbishop did not mention specific details to White, he seemed to be aware of "the imminence of the situation," saying: "I only hope that when they kill me they don't kill many of us."[6] He had no idea how the assassin might strike, but he knew it would be violent, like Rutilio's killing, and he did not want any innocents injured or killed because they refused to cease watching and waiting with him.

During what turned out to be his last newspaper interview, this one with the Mexican newspaper *Excelsior* just two weeks before his death, Romero talked about the martyrdom that many feared was rushing toward their beloved archbishop. "I have frequently been threatened with death. I ought to say that, as a Christian, I do not believe in death without resurrection. If they kill me I will rise again in the people of El Salvador. I am not boasting, I say it with the greatest humility. I am bound, as a pastor, by a divine command to give my life for those whom I love, and that is all Salvadorans, even those who are going to kill me. If they manage to carry out their threats, from this moment I offer my blood for the redemption and resurrection of El Salvador."

Romero called martyrdom "a grace from God which I do not believe I deserve."

"But if God accepts the sacrifice of my life," he said, "then may my blood be the seed of liberty, and a sign of hope that will soon become a reality. May my death . . . be for the liberation of my people, and as a witness of hope in what is to come. Can you tell them, if they succeed in killing me, that I pardon and bless those who do it? But I wish that they could realize that they are wasting their time. A bishop may die, but the church of God, which is the people, will never die."[7]

And he urged his people on to continue the struggle in the event of his death. "If some day they take the radio station away from us, if they close down our newspaper, if they don't let us speak, if they kill all the priests and the bishop, too, and you are left, a people without priests, each one of you must be God's microphone, each one of you must be a messenger, a prophet," Romero had told them. "The church will always exist as long as there is one baptized person. And that one baptized person who is left in the world is responsible before the world for holding aloft the banner of the Lord's truth and of his divine justice."

On March 23, 1980, technicians working overtime with an anxious archbishop looking over their shoulders were finally able to return YSAX to the airwaves after a bomb had destroyed its transmitter five weeks earlier. They completed the job just in time to broadcast Romero's fearless, historic denunciation of the nation's military oppression, his heartfelt call to "brothers" among the enlisted men in the armed forces, "who kill your own campesino brothers and sisters."

Romero's message was heard, its danger assessed by Roberto D'Aubuisson and the people who goaded or directed him (who have never been identified), and their plans were made and the next day executed. It did not take a lot to plan a murder in those days with so many people and materials already on hand to do the job. The men of the death squads had long ago gotten over whatever superstitions they might have had about killing a priest. Now they were even ready to kill a bishop, even one standing before an altar.

"I was only ten feet away, sitting on the second pew on the east side, when Monseñor was shot," a Carmelite sister said, recalling the assassination many years later. "We were very attentive to the moment, as he finished his homily. Then a shot rang out. It was a strange sound, perhaps because the microphone and the light were nearby. It sounded like a bomb had exploded. He fell to the ground immediately.

"It's strange," she said. "I didn't feel afraid. Instead, I felt courage and ran immediately to help Monseñor. But seeing the tremendous hemorrhage of blood flowing from his nose, mouth and ears, and realizing I couldn't do anything, my first reaction was to look in the direction of the main door of the chapel from where the shot had been fired. I wanted to see who had done this, but I didn't see anybody.

"At that point I realized that God had heard Monseñor's prayer. He always said that if such a thing were to occur, he hoped nobody else would be affected. The truth is, we all expected that this would happen one day; but we never imagined that anybody would dare commit such a sacrilege and kill him at the very moment he celebrated the Eucharist. If we look at it from the perspective of the people, perhaps it was better that way. Martyrdom is not granted to just any person, but only to those who are worthy of it. Monseñor was a saint, and his whole life was a great witness. So it was a crowning prize for him, especially since it happened at the altar.

"It were as though the Lord had spoken to him: 'I don't want you just to offer me bread. Now you are the victim, you are my offering.' "[8]

CONCLUSION

The Deluge

The astonishing spectacle of the assassination of an archbishop was quickly followed by the astonishing spectacle of his funeral.

Prelates and priests had come from all over Europe, the United States, and Central and South America to pay their respects to the murdered archbishop on Palm Sunday, March 30, 1980, a week after Romero had been slain before the altar. Of his brother bishops of the Salvadoran conference, only his ally Bishop Rivera would appear at Romero's funeral Mass.

The funeral ceremonies started calmly with a procession of thirty bishops, followed by more than two hundred priests to the Metropolitan Cathedral. Thousands of mourners, campesinos from the countryside and professionals from the city, people from all corners of Salvadoran life, pressed into the church from the plaza outside. People, even old men and women, had walked for days from the far ends of El Salvador, too poor to travel otherwise, just so they could be there to visit with the Monseñor one more time.

The foreign clergy who had come to honor the fallen archbishop had been assured that the day would pass peacefully. Leaders of the Popular Front vowed to observe nonviolence in honor of the archbishop, and, according to an American priest who participated in the funeral "it seemed unthinkable that the hard-line right would desecrate this moment unless first provoked."[1]

And so it seemed at first with more than two hundred and fifty thousand gathered to remember Romero inside the cathedral and in the square before it and streets around it. "All went peacefully through a succession of prayers, readings, hymns," James Connor, SJ, a concelebrant at the funeral, wrote, "until the moment in his homily when Cardinal Ernesto Corripio Ahumada of Mexico, the personal delegate of Pope John Paul II, began to praise Archbishop Romero as a man of peace and a foe of violence."

Referencing one of Romero's well-known teachings, Corripio said, "Violence cannot kill truth or justice. We cannot love by hating. We cannot defend life by killing."

As if to mock his words, a bomb exploded outside the cathedral at the far edge of the plaza, near the front of the National Palace. "Next, gun shots, sharp and clear, echoed off the walls surrounding the plaza," wrote Connor. "At first, the cardinal's plea for all to remain calm seemed to have a steadying impact. But as another explosion reverberated, panic took hold and the crowd broke ranks and ran. Some headed for the side streets, but thousands more rushed up the stairs and fought their way into the cathedral." And there they would remain for hours waiting for the violence outside to subside.[2]

Connor wondered how long it would be before a grenade were thrown directly into the cathedral where the peasants were huddled together, or if a gunman might appear in a cathedral entrance to strafe the crowd. "I watched the terrified mob push through the doors until every inch of space was filled," he wrote. "Looking about me, I suddenly realized that, aside from the nuns, priests, and bishops, the mourners were the poor and the powerless of El Salvador. Absent were government representatives of the nation or of other countries." As the sound of explosions grew closer, he wondered, were they all going to be killed?

And so it continued for the next two hours as the wounded and the dead from the streets outside were brought into the cathedral. As the violence persisted outside, somehow Romero's coffin was moved to the inside of the cathedral, and Cardinal Corripio and others hastily buried Romero in the tomb that had been prepared in the east transept of the cathedral.

Finally the papal nuncio to El Salvador received assurance by phone "from some government source" that it was safe for the people to leave. Those who had been trapped inside filed out into the street with hands raised, per the instructions given the nuncio, "so as to assure any potential snipers that we were unarmed."[3]

Witnesses said that Salvadoran soldiers threw the bombs into the crowd; others claimed to see army sharpshooters on rooftops surrounding the cathedral. The government blamed "leftists" for the violence. For many who had hoped for a peaceful resolution to the tensions in Salvadoran society, the killing of Romero and now this obscenity outside the Metropolitan Cathedral were the last straws. These crimes in the plaza, like the killing of Romero and the murders of thousands of others over the next decade, were never "solved" by the government.

It is hard to overstate how tragic the loss of Oscar Romero would prove to be for the people of El Salvador on both sides of the political and economic chasm that divided the nation. Roberto D'Aubuisson and the other men who

conspired to rid El Salvador of this priest believed that killing Romero would somehow put an end to the agitation
taking place among the poor they had long presumed should
remain completely at their disposal and within their control.
But killing Romero achieved the opposite outcome. The
people in the countryside deeply believed in Romero as their
protector and their hope. With his death entire communities
turned their allegiance over to the guerrilla forces that were
then organizing. They did not "give up," as much as they
gave up on the idea that change in El Salvador could come
at the ballot instead of at the barrelhead of an AK-47.

Many urban moderates, still hoping they could work
within the shambles of the Salvadoran democratic process,
saw the killing of Romero as the end for peaceful change.
The armed groups themselves perceived the killing of Romero
and its aftermath as the signal to ratchet up their armed
struggle, not abandon it, coming together finally into a united
front through the Farabundo Martí National Liberation
Front (in Spanish, Frente Farabundo Martí para la Libera-
ción Nacional or FMLN) just a few months after Romero
was gunned down.

But of course the ones whose tragedy would be greatest
in the aftermath of the slaying of Romero were the simple
people of El Salvador he had died to protect, people not
necessarily seeking social change through armed struggle or
in any other manner of struggle; survival was their struggle.
They remained exquisitely vulnerable, and they were time
after time punished for that vulnerability.

"Violence was a fire that swept over the fields of El Salvador, it burst into villages, cut off roads and destroyed
highways and bridges, energy sources and transmission
lines; it reached the cities and entered families, sacred areas
and educational centers; it struck at justice and filled the

public administration with victims; and it singled out as an enemy anyone who was not on the list of friends. Violence turned everything to death and destruction . . ."⁴ This is the rather poetic introduction of the UN Truth Commission's report on El Salvador. It would be reassuring to regard that description as an author's hyperbolic flight, but in truth the opening paragraphs of the commission's findings merely capture the horrific violent rush of the years that followed pastor Oscar Romero's death. His killing marked a stark turn for the worst in El Salvador. It was as if those most responsible for the violence had turned to their brothers and sisters in Salvadoran society and said: see, we have killed the archbishop; we are capable of any depravity now.

Over the following two years, thirty-five thousand Salvadorans would die in the violence that would engulf the country; fifteen percent of the population fled into exile; thousands simply "disappeared." The conflict dragged on until 1992, when both sides, exhausted by the by-now pointless struggle, agreed to a ceasefire and security guarantees that allowed the FMLN's political resistance to transform itself into disarmed political parties with a stake in a peaceful electoral process. Taking up a responsibility long abandoned by Salvadoran government, the UN Truth Commission would eventually affix blame for more than eighty-five percent of the extra-judicial killings on the Salvadoran military (five percent was attributed to the FMLN and ten percent declared undetermined).

In San Salvador after some delay, Arturo Rivera replaced Romero as archbishop, who followed much the same progressive course as his predecessor, if more cautiously. Archbishops who have succeeded Rivera, however, have been notably resistant to the pastoral style and political direction set by Romero. The current archbishop, José Luis Escobar

Alas, caused widespread outrage in El Salvador when in September 2013 he abruptly closed Romero's legal aid office (now called Tutela Legal), issuing a statement that claimed its work was "no longer relevant." Many have challenged that decision, suggesting the office was closed to prevent its thousands of documents on human rights abuses from getting in the hands of new investigations into the many human rights abuses of the war.

In May 1980 Major Robert D'Aubuisson and some associates were arrested on his farm in Santa Tecla, accused of plotting a coup against the faltering junta. Evidence connecting him to the killing of Romero was discovered on the farm, but to the end D'Aubuisson denied any role in Romero's murder. His arrest triggered a wave of right-wing violence. He was eventually released, and efforts to persecute him abandoned. D'Aubuisson would never be formally charged in connection with the assassination of the archbishop, and he would never be called on to testify about the men he directed or the men who directed him in the Romero plot. He would go on to become one of the founders in 1981 of the right-wing ARENA party (Nationalist Republican Alliance or Alianza Republicana). ARENA, with the help of the United States, would control the government of El Salvador for decades, both during and after the civil war.

In 2009 when the FMLN finally wrested control of the government—peacefully—from ARENA, its leaders hailed the inspiration they drew from Romero's martyrdom. After winning the presidency, FMLN candidate Mauricio Funes said, "I will govern like Monseñor Romero wanted the men of his time to govern with courage, but with prophetic vision. Bishop Romero asked the rulers to listen to the cry of justice from the Salvadoran people."

The bishop, as he had always said he would be, was resurrected in the life of la puebla, his people, who have never forgotten him. In death his influence was even more keenly felt throughout El Salvador and among the poor whose struggle for peace and justice was not deterred by the killing of Romero that evening decades ago. It continues to this day.

Since the end of the civil war, El Salvador has remained one of the most violent societies in the hemisphere. Poverty persists, but the death squads that haunt the nights of San Salvador today have more to do with drug trafficking than political repression. El Salvador is still struggling with many of the unresolved political and economic conflicts of Romero's time and struggling to accept the radical solidarity and sharing preached by the martyred archbishop.

"Peace is not the product of terror or fear," Romero said. "Peace is not the silence of cemeteries. Peace is not the silent result of violent repression. Peace is the generous, tranquil contribution of all to the good of all. Peace is dynamism. Peace is generosity. It is right, and it is duty. In it each one has a place in this beautiful family, which the Epiphany brightens for us with God's light."

That is the peace that El Salvador still reaches for, and while it does, alongside his country's people, as posters and graffiti throughout the capital attest to this day: *Romero vive.*

Notes

Introduction—pages 1–14

1. James R. Brockman, SJ, *Romero: A Life* (Maryknoll, NY: Orbis Books, 2005), 169–70.
2. Oscar Romero, *A Shepherd's Diary*, trans. Irene Hodgson, (Washington: USCC, 1993), 214–15.
3. Ibid., 125.
4. Oscar Romero, "Christ, An Always New Word for the Church," homily for February 18, 1979, http://www.romerotrust.org.uk /homilies/141/141_pdf.pdf.
5. *El pueblo es mi profeta*, http://www.youtube.com/watch?v =2GDdFW62BbA.
6. Cindy Wooden, "Magazine Says Archbishop Romero Was Killed for Actions of Faith," Catholic News Service, November 4, 2005, http://www.catholicnews.com/data/stories/cns/0506300.htm.
7. Pat Marrin, "Oscar Romero Sainthood Cause on Long, Tangled Path," *National Catholic Reporter*, May 10, 2013, http://ncronline .org/news/people/sainthood-cause-long-tangled-path.
8. Roberto Cuéllar, "Monseñor Oscar Romero: Human Rights Apostle," in *Monsignor Romero: A Bishop for the Third Millennium*, ed. Robert S. Pelton, CSC (Notre Dame: University of Notre Dame Press, 2004), 46.

Chapter One: Death Comes for the Archbishop— pages 15–26

1. UN Truth Commission, "From Madness to Hope: the 12-Year War in El Salvador" (United States Institute of Peace, January 26, 2001), 122.

2. Romero, "Last Homily of Archbishop Romero: March 24, 1980," trans. James Brockman, in *Voice of the Voiceless: The Four Pastoral Letters and Other Statements* (Maryknoll, NY: Orbis Books, 1985), 191–92.

3. Ibid., 192–93.

4. Carlos Dada, "How We Killed Archbishop Romero," *El Faro*, March 25, 2010, http://www.elfaro.net/es/201003/noticias/1416.

5. Ibid.

6. Ibid.

7. Jon Sobrino, *Archbishop Romero: Memories and Reflections* (Eugene, OR: Wipf and Stock, 2004), 41.

8. Andrew Buncombe, "The Archbishop, the Death Squad and the 24-year Wait for Justice," *The Independent* (August 24, 2004), http://www.independent.co.uk/news/world/americas/the-archbishop-the-death-squad-and-the-24year-wait-for-justice-6163208.html.

9. James LeMoyne, "Picture of Death Squads Seen in Key Salvadoran Notebook," *New York Times* (December 2, 1987), http://www.nytimes.com/1987/12/02/world/picture-of-death-squads-seen-in-key-salvadoran-notebook.html.

10. Dada, "How We Killed Archbishop Romero."

Chapter Two: Romero's El Salvador—pages 27–37

1. Romero, "Last Homily of Archbishop Romero: March 24, 1980," 55.

2. Ibid., 4.

3. Ibid., 33.

4. Ibid.

5. Ibid., 36.

6. Ibid.

7. María López Vigil, *Monseñor Romero: Memories in Mosaic* (Maryknoll, NY: Orbis Books, 2013), 4.

8. Office for the Canonization of Oscar Romero, Archdiocese of San Salvador, *Monseñor Romero: Un Misterio de Dios*, dir. by Guillermo Gomez and Oscar Orellana, posted March 24, 2012, http://www.youtube.com/watch?v=QRdZuFHzhng.

9. Damian Zynda, *Archbishop Oscar Romero: A Disciple Who Revealed the Glory of God* (Scranton, NJ: University of Scranton Press, 2010), 6.

10. Jeffrey M. Paige, *Coffee and Power: Revolution and the Rise of Democracy in Central America* (Cambridge: Harvard University Press, 1997), Chapter 1, "Revolution and the Coffee Elite."

11. Ibid., 103.

12. Ibid., 31.

13. Ibid.

Chapter Three: The Young Priest—pages 38–57

1. James R. Brockman, SJ, "The Spiritual Journey of Oscar Romero," *Spirituality Today*, Winter 1990, vol. 42, no. 4, 303–22, http://www.spiritualitytoday.org/spir2day/904242brock.html#15.

2. Ibid.

3. Brockman, *Romero: A Life*, 37.

4. Ibid., 38.

5. Ibid., 40.

6. Ibid.

7. López Vigil, *Monseñor Romero*, 6.

8. Ibid., 10–11.

9. Ibid., 10.

10. Ibid., 7.

11. Zynda, *Archbishop Oscar Romero*, 14.

12. López Vigil, *Monseñor Romero*, 12.

13. Ibid., 19.

14. Brockman, *Romero: A Life,* 23.

15. Zynda, *Archbishop Oscar Romero*, 24.

16. López Vigil, *Monseñor Romero*, 23.

17. Ibid., 25.

18. Ibid., 25–27.

19. Brockman, *Romero: A Life,* 51–52.

Chapter Four: The Cautious Cleric—pages 58–67

1. López Vigil, *Monseñor Romero*, 33.
2. Brockman, *Romero: A Life*, 52.
3. López Vigil, *Monseñor Romero*, 39.
4. Brockman, *Romero: A Life*, 59.
5. Ibid., 60.
6. Roberto Cuéllar, "Monseñor Oscar Romero: Human Rights Apostle," 9.
7. Edmundo Moran, "El Salvador's Climate of Terror," *America* 138, no. 6 (February 18, 1978): 117–19.
8. Rubén Zamora, "The Empowering Spirit of Archbishop Romero: A Personal Testimony," in Pelton, *Monsignor Romero*, 48.
9. Enrique Dussel, *A History of the Church in Latin America: Colonialism to Liberation (1492–1979)* (Grand Rapids, MI: Wm B. Eerdmans, 1981), 227.
10. López Vigil, *Monseñor Romero*, 40–41.
11. Ibid., 41.
12. Ibid., 42.

Chapter Five: Shepherd of His People—pages 68–88

1. Ignacio Martín-Baró, "Oscar Romero: Voice of the Downtrodden," in Romero, *Voice of the Voiceless*, 4.
2. López Vigil, *Monseñor Romero*, 51.
3. Brockman, *Romero: A Life*, 56–58.
4. Roberto Cuéllar, "Monseñor Oscar Romero: Human Rights Apostle," 7.
5. López Vigil, *Monseñor Romero*, 60.
6. Martín-Baró, 5.
7. Cuéllar, "Monseñor Oscar Romero," 6.
8. López Vigil, "Bishop Romero's Baptism by the People," "Oscar Romero," http://www.envio.org.ni/articulo/1675.
9. Brockman, *Romero: A Life*, 6.
10. López Vigil, *Monseñor Romero*, 64–65.
11. Ibid., 17.
12. Ibid.

13. Ibid., 6.

14. Dean Brackley, SJ, "Rutilio and Romero: Martyrs for Our Time" in Pelton, *Monsignor Romero*, 82.

15. Sobrino, *Archbishop Romero*, 4.

16. Alan Riding, "Latin Church in Siege," *New York Times Magazine* (May 6, 1979): 236.

17. López Vigil, *Monseñor Romero*, 67.

18. Sobrino, *Archbishop Romero*, 10.

19. Ibid., 8.

20. Ibid., 6–7.

21. Brockman, *Romero: A Life*, 10.

22. Brackley, "Rutilio and Romero," 92.

23. López Vigil, *Monseñor Romero*, 78.

Chapter Six: A Nation in Crisis—pages 89–99

1. Brockman, *Romero: A Life*, 144.

2. Joseph Nangle, OFM, "Archbishop Romero's Challenge to U.S. Universities," in Pelton, *Monsignor Romero*, 103.

3. López Vigil, *Monseñor Romero*, 109.

4. Ibid., 106.

5. Brockman, *Romero: A Life*, 21.

6. Ibid., 22.

7. Ibid.

8. López Vigil, *Monseñor Romero*, 104.

9. Brockman, *Romero: A Life*, 162.

10. Romero, *A Shepherd's Diary*, 335.

Chapter Seven: Love, the Vengeance of Christians— pages 100–116

1. Romero, "The Strength of Prayer," homily for July 17, 1977, http://www.romerotrust.org.uk/homilies/34/34_pdf.pdf.

2. López Vigil, *Monseñor Romero*, 113.

3. Organization of American States, Chapter 2: "Right to Life" in "Report on the Situation of Human Rights in El Salvador," November 17, 1978, http://www.cidh.org/countryrep/ElSalvador78eng /chap.2.htm.

4. Brackley, "Rutilio and Romero," 92.

5. López Vigil, *Monseñor Romero*, 117.

6. Ibid., 201.

7. Alma Guillermoprieto, "Death Comes for the Archbishop," *The New York Review of Books*, http://www.nybooks.com/articles /archives/2010/may/27/death-comes-archbishop.

8. Brockman, *Romero: A Life*, 176.

9. Romero, "The Good Shepherd," homily for April 16, 1978, http://www.romerotrust.org.uk/homilies/95/95_pdf.pdf.

10. Marie Dennis, Renny Golden, Scott Wright, *Oscar Romero, Reflections on His Life and Writings* (Maryknoll, NY: Orbis, 2000), 23.

Chapter Eight: The *Locura*—pages 117–30

1. López Vigil, *Monseñor Romero*, 102.

2. Brockman, *Romero: A Life*, 190.

3. Alma Guillermoprieto, "Remembering Romero: The Murder that Ruptured El Salvador," NYR Blog: Roving Thoughts and Provocations (blog), *The New York Review of Books*, April 22, 2010, http://www.nybooks.com/blogs/nyrblog/2010/apr/22/remembering -romero-murder-ruptured-el-salvador.

4. Romero, *A Shepherd's Diary*, 176.

5. Ibid., 493.

6. Inter-american Commission on Human Rights, Organization of American States, "Report no. 37/00, case 11.481, Monsignor Oscar Arnulfo Romero y Galdámez, El Salvador," April 13, 2000, http:// www.cidh.oas.org/annualrep/99eng/Merits/ElSalvador11.481.htm.

7. Luciano Mendes de Alameida, SJ, "Martyrs, Heroes, and the Contemporary Church: Latin America and the United States," in Pelton, *Monsignor Romero*, 31.

8. This quote appears in the Religious Task Force on Central America and Mexico's *Central America/Mexico Report: Archbishop Oscar Romero*, January/February 2005, 15, http://www.marquette .edu/cm/justice/documents/25anniversary.pdf.

Conclusion: The Deluge—pages 131–37

1. James L. Connor, SJ, "A Report from Romero's Funeral," *America* magazine, April 26, 1980, http://americamagazine.org /issue/100/report-romeros-funeral.

2. Ibid.

3. Ibid.

4. UN Truth Commission, "From Madness to Hope: The 12-Year War in El Salvador" (United States Institute of Peace, January 26, 2001), 10.

Bibliography

Brackley, Dean, SJ. "Rutilio and Romero: Martyrs for Our Time." In Pelton, *Monsignor Romero,* 79–100.

Brockman, James R., SJ. *Romero: A Life.* Maryknoll, NY: Orbis Books, 2005.

———. "The Spiritual Journey of Oscar Romero." *Spirituality Today* 42, no. 4 (1990): 303–22. http://www.spiritualitytoday.org /spir2day/904242brock.html#15.

Buncombe, Andrew. "The Archbishop, the Death Squad and the 24-year Wait for Justice." *The Independent* (August 24, 2004). http://www.independent.co.uk/news/world/americas /the-archbishop-the-death-squad-and-the-24year-wait-for -justice-6163208.html.

Connor, James L., SJ. "A Report from Romero's Funeral." *America,* April 26, 1980, http://americamagazine.org/issue/100 /report-romeros-funeral.

Cuéllar, Roberto M. "Monseñor Oscar Romero: Human Rights Apostle." In Pelton, *Monsignor Romero,* 35–46.

Dada, Carlos. "How We Killed Archbishop Romero." *El Faro,* March 25, 2010, http://www.elfaro.net/es/201003 /noticias/1416.

Dennis, Marie, Renny Golden, and Scott Wright. *Oscar Romero, Reflections on His Life and Writings.* Modern Spiritual Masters Series. Maryknoll, NY: Orbis, 2000.

Dussel, Enrique. *A History of the Church in Latin America: Colonialism to Liberation (1492–1979).* Grand Rapids, MI: Wm B. Eerdmans, 1981.

Guillermoprieto, Alma. "Death Comes for the Archbishop." *The New York Review of Books*, May 27, 2010, http://www.nybooks.com/articles/archives/2010/may/27/death-comes-archbishop.

———. "Remembering Romero: The Murder that Ruptured El Salvador." NYR Blog: Roving Thoughts and Provocations (blog). *The New York Review of Books*, April 22, 2010, http://www.nybooks.com/blogs/nyrblog/2010/apr/22/remembering-romero-murder-ruptured-el-salvador.

Inter-american Commission on Human Rights, Organization of American States. "Report no. 37/00, case 11.481, Monsignor Oscar Arnulfo Romero y Galdámez, El Salvador." April 13, 2000. http://www.cidh.oas.org/annualrep/99eng/Merits/ElSalvador11.481.htm.

LeMoyne, James. "Picture of Death Squads Seen in Key Salvadoran Notebook." *New York Times*, December 2, 1987, http://www.nytimes.com/1987/12/02/world/picture-of-death-squads-seen-in-key-salvadoran-notebook.html.

López Vigil, María. "Bishop Romero's Baptism by the People." *Envio* 139, April 1993, http://www.envio.org.ni/articulo/1675.

———. *Monseñor Romero: Memories in Mosaic*. Maryknoll, NY: Orbis, 2013.

Marrin, Pat. "Oscar Romero Sainthood Cause on Long, Tangled Path." *National Catholic Reporter*, May 10, 2013, http://ncronline.org/news/people/sainthood-cause-long-tangled-path.

Martín-Baró, Ignacio. "Oscar Romero: Voice of the Downtrodden." In Romero, *Voice of the Voiceless*, 1–21.

Mendes de Almeida, Luciano, SJ. "Martyrs, Heroes, and the Contemporary Church: Latin America and the United States." In Pelton, *Monsignor Romero*, 27–34.

Moran, Edmundo. "El Salvador's Climate of Terror." *America* 138, no. 6, February 18, 1978, 117–19.

Nangle, Joseph, OFM. "Archbishop Romero's Challenge to U.S. Universities." In Pelton, *Monsignor Romero*, 101–12.

Office for the Canonization of Oscar Romero, Archdiocese of San Salvador. "Monseñor Romero: Un Misterio de Dios." Directed by Guillermo Gomez and Oscar Orellana. Posted March 24, 2012. http://www.youtube.com/watch?v =QRdZuFHzhng.

Organization of American States. "Report on the Situation of Human Rights in El Salvador." November 17, 1978, http:// www.cidh.org/countryrep/elsalvador78eng/toc.htm.

Paige, Jeffrey M. *Coffee and Power: Revolution and the Rise of Democracy in Central America.* Cambridge: Harvard University Press, 1997.

Pelton, Robert S., CSC, ed. *Monsignor Romero: A Bishop for the Third Millennium.* Notre Dame: University of Notre Dame Press, 2004.

Religious Task Force on Central America and Mexico. *Central America/Mexico Report: Archbishop Oscar Romero,* January/February 2005, http://www.marquette.edu/cm /justice/documents/25anniversary.pdf.

Riding, Alan. "Latin Church in Siege." *New York Times Magazine,* May 6, 1979, 236.

Romero, Oscar. "Christ, An Always New Word for the Church." Homily for February 18, 1979, http://www.romerotrust .org.uk/homilies/141/141_pdf.pdf.

———. "The Good Shepherd." Homily for April 16, 1978, http:// www.romerotrust.org.uk/homilies/95/95_pdf.pdf.

———. *A Shepherd's Diary.* Translated by Irene Hodgson. Washington: USCC, 1993.

———. "The Strength of Prayer." Homily for July 17, 1977, http:// www.romerotrust.org.uk/homilies/34/34_pdf.pdf.

———. *Voice of the Voiceless: The Four Pastoral Letters and Other Statements.* Maryknoll, NY: Orbis Books, 1985.

Sobrino, Jon. *Archbishop Romero: Memories and Reflections.* Eugene, OR: Wipf and Stock, 2004.

UN Truth Commission. "From Madness to Hope: The 12-Year War in El Salvador." United States Institute of Peace, January 26, 2001.

Wooden, Cindy. "Magazine Says Archbishop Romero Was Killed for Actions of Faith." Catholic News Service, November 4, 2005, http://www.catholicnews.com/data/stories /cns/0506300.htm.

Zamora, Rubén. "The Empowering Spirit of Archbishop Romero: A Personal Testimony." In Pelton, *Monsignor Romero,* 47–50.

Zynda, Damian. *Archbishop Oscar Romero: A Disciple Who Revealed the Glory of God.* Scranton, NJ: University of Scranton Press, 2010.

Index